Com~~~

Australian Birds

ALAN BELL

with drawings
by
SHIRLEY BELL

MELBOURNE

OXFORD UNIVERSITY PRESS

LONDON WELLINGTON NEW YORK

*Oxford University Press, Ely House, London, W.*1

GLASGOW NEW YORK TORONTO MELBOURNE WELLINGTON
CAPE TOWN SALISBURY IBADAN NAIROBI LUSAKA ADDIS ABABA
BOMBAY CALCUTTA MADRAS KARACHI LAHORE DACCA
KUALA LUMPUR SINGAPORE HONG KONG TOKYO

Oxford University Press, 7 Bowen Crescent, Melbourne

SBN 19 550043 1

First published 1956
Revised edition 1969

Registered in Australia for transmission by post as a book
PRINTED AT THE GRIFFIN PRESS, MARION ROAD, NETLEY, S.A.

COMMON
AUSTRALIAN BIRDS

CONTENTS

In Orders and Families

SMALL BIRDS

LARGE BIRDS

vii

INTRODUCTION

THIS book is designed to help people in the more closely settled parts of Australia to recognize birds they may see at home in the garden or during a day's outing. Of more than 650 native birds, just over a hundred are included; they are the 'probables' for observers who may not contemplate hunts after distant species or working through the full Australian list to identify local birds.

The title will seem more satisfactory in some regions than in others. Certainly the birds 'common' for fifty miles around Brisbane will differ from those near Adelaide. But the selection was made after the author had taken notes in all parts of the country except along stretches of the western coastline, and it is hoped that not many of the right candidates have been omitted.

The side-by-side descriptions and illustrations have not been made infinitely detailed. They aim at a quick identification by word and picture. Then follows a short section to convey something of each bird's habits and 'personality'.

Arrangement

The birds have been divided into two groups: Small Birds, whose length from bill tip to end of tail feathers usually measures ten inches or less; and Large Birds, those normally of ten inches or more in length. Generally, small birds are illustrated at half-size and large birds at one-quarter or one-eighth size, but variations have been made in both groups owing to the considerable range of bird sizes. The natural size and the reduction of each bird are given below each illustration.

The opening paragraph on each bird, *Recognition*, gives its range and the impression it would leave at a brief encounter. The type of country where it is likely to be found is given by a figure at the end of the paragraph. The figures signify: (1) Open, (2) Wooded, (3) Fresh water, (4) Sea and shore, (5) Settlements and gardens.

The second paragraph, *Description*, gives the bird's size in inches and its plumage colours.

The final paragraph amplifies the description with comments on the bird's character, habits, manners and usefulness.

A number of authorities have been good enough to scrutinize text and illustrations. Especially I should like to thank Mr Alec H. Chisholm and Mr Vincent Serventy, who respectively checked what is said of birds on the eastern and western sides of Australia.

A. B.

Introduction to the Second Edition

It has been possible to include four extra birds from among those which readers report they would have liked to have had covered. Some birds have been re-drawn; but the main difference in the new edition is that much additional information is offered on the hundred or so birds originally chosen. The further comments on appearance and manners will, I hope, enable still more positive and rapid identification.

A. B.

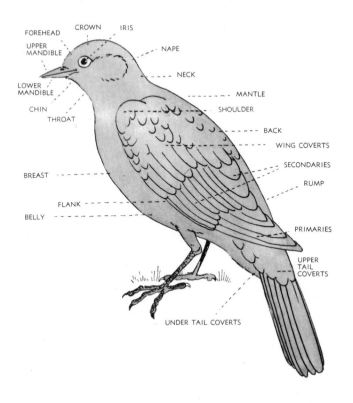

ANATOMICAL DIAGRAM OF A BIRD

SMALL BIRDS

Birds of less than ten inches from bill tip to end of tail feathers. Birds in this section are reproduced generally to one-half natural size.

BLUE WREN *Malurus cyaneus*

RECOGNITION: Southern Q'ld, Vic., S.A., Tas. Long tail carried at right-angle; scintillating blue and black; usually on ground; (2,5)

DESCRIPTION: 5. Crown, cheeks, upper back bright blue, tail darker blue; nape, breast, lower back black; abdomen and undertail white; wings brown; legs and bill black; iris brown. *Female* and *young males* brown, under parts lighter; bill, and around eye reddish-brown.

These minute, intensely coloured birds were among the first to be noted by Australia's discoverers. There are fourteen species of the same general form—red, black, purple and varying blues; but several are almost unknown outside museums. The Blue Wren is abundant in the eastern States and the Variegated and Red-backed Wrens are not uncommon northward from Victoria. Blue Wrens are mostly seen on the ground, where their agility makes up for weak flying powers. The tail, stiffly balanced aloft, strikes one immediately; it about equals the length of the body. The blue and black feathers have the sheeny depth of fine, richly-dyed velvet. Often one of these atoms of polished elegance, as he hunts the undergrowth and runs down insects, is shepherded by three or four soberly-feathered brown wrens—a concourse of wives, it has been suggested, but more probably the current brood, a family of females and young males. For three or four seasons the blue mating plumage is impermanent and reverts with the moult to brown. The trilling song, daintily emphatic and magnified by the darkness, sometimes breaks out in spring and summer nights.

BLUE WREN

NATURAL SIZE 5″   *Reproduced about 2/3 natural size*

YELLOW-TAILED THORNBILL *Acanthiza chrysorrhoa*

RECOGNITION: Aus., except north-western, N.T. and Tas. Usually feeds on ground; distinctive gold rump. (2,5)

DESCRIPTION: 4¾. Upper parts olive-brown; rump strong yellow; tail, terminal black band; forehead darker, spotted white; whitish line over eye; under parts soiled white, buff on flanks; legs and bill black; iris grey.

The Yellow-tailed Thornbill may appear the most common thornbill because it can hardly be overlooked; as it drops to cover the eye picks up the bright rump plainly, as though a sovereign had gone spinning into the ditch. Small winter flocks, which sometimes include other thornbill species, ferret along hedges, outskirts of woods and through gardens; the minute size of the birds and their quick, acrobatic examination of twigs for insects remind New Australians of the Tom-Tit, everybody's favourite in Europe. An impatient 'Chip-chip' is the call that keeps the flock in touch and the song, a lively little run of notes, is audible in most months. The birds are usually noticed rather low, in, or very close to, cover. The nest, which may be about head-high in a clump of leaves on a branch, is worth hunting for. It is a domed structure, comfortably lined, with a porch-like entry on one side and a second storey, or false nest, not so well finished, above. The loft shows few signs of use. Both birds build, but the male does not share in incubation; and one of the unsatisfactory speculations put forward is that the cock takes a bed in the upper 'dressing-room' while his mate is hatching her eggs on the floor below. This is the equal of a further theory—that visiting cuckoos will overlook the breeding chamber proper and leave their eggs to cool in the penthouse.

YELLOW-TAILED THORNBILL

NATURAL SIZE $4\frac{3}{4}''$ *Reproduced about 2/3 natural size*

STRIATED THORNBILL *Acanthiza lineata*

RECOGNITION: Southern Q'ld to S.A. Light throat and chest, pencilled darker; minute, active. (2,5)

DESCRIPTION: 3½. Back olive-brown; head brown, streaked lighter; throat and chest soiled white with blackish lines; flanks and belly yellowish; legs and bill brown; iris whitish.

Active, sharp, industriously prying, hardly a fork or cranny of bush or tree is too cramped for the Striated Thornbill to investigate. Its life seems one long, rapid inspection and its appetite for moths, spiders, insects and their larvae is never satisfied. It must be a perennial destroyer of the lesser enemies of trees and plants. The hunt goes on in company; miniature rustlings and whirrings—and the chattering the flocks keep up—may be the first hints that a party is foraging near by. The in-and-out procession will work its way along a hedge or pass over high in the foliage of the trees. The Striated Thornbills, so obsessed by business, attract by their adept, methodical and tradesman-like ways. At close quarters the reticent colouring, with its streaks and freckling, is modestly pleasing. The nest, an oval of grass well-laced with cobwebs and lined with feathers, lichen and soft materials, is built with characteristic thoroughness. The entrance is hooded and the height at which it is placed among tree-twigs varies considerably. At the moment the Thornbill group is allowed seventeen species, but a numerous community of small birds which presents puzzling cross-references still encourages research by classifiers.

STRIATED THORNBILL

NATURAL SIZE $3\frac{1}{2}''$ *Reproduced about 2/3 natural size*

REED WARBLER *Acrocephalus australis*

RECOGNITION: Aus. Loud calls, alternately harsh and silvery; active brown percher in reeds. (3)

DESCRIPTION: 7. Upper parts warm brown, deeper on primaries and tail; distinct, pale eyestreak; under parts silvery buff; throat white; legs grey; bill and iris brown.

It is worth surveying expanses of reeds to see whether this warbler has settled in. Its nest is a craftsman's construction, a safe cylinder for eggs and young, made of reeds and appended to three or more standing or growing stems, with balance and enough play to offset every shake of wind. Usually the bird's insistent song tells whether a reed forest is inhabited. This song is of mixed quality. Grunting notes, produced hesitantly and as if with effort, break through to silvery calls, strong, cheerful and clear, with phrases at moments reminiscent of the English thrush. The singing—as, for example, in Strathalbyn, South Australia—may become the day and night music of a town. The warblers take no heed of a park seat near their nests. Their colouring blends with the grey straw of last year's reeds, but commotion among the stems indicates their restless explorations. A slim brown form will be glimpsed presently in a rapid traverse, or seen near a stem top, leaning aside at an angle and flinging out a burst of song. Water and flying insects, caterpillars and the like are briskly chased. The migratory movements of the European race are still not wholly clear and the seasonal advents of the Australian Reed Warbler need further study. In the south-east the birds are apparently absent between April and August.

REED WARBLER

NATURAL SIZE 7″   *Reproduced about 1/2 natural size*

SPOTTED DIAMOND BIRD   *Pardalotus punctatus*

RECOGNITION: Aust. except N.T. and Central. 'Sleep, my baby' call, soothingly monotonous; tiny, stumpy, white-spotted. (2)

DESCRIPTION: 3¼. Back grey-buff, spotted black; crown, wings and tail black, spotted white; rump chestnut; tail coverts fiery red; white eyebrow; throat and undertail, gay yellow; abdomen fawn; legs flesh-colour; bill black; iris grey. *Female*, yellow spots replace white; less yellow under tail.

When this tiny, hectic bird is mining at a bank, clearing a foot or more of tunnel for the nest, it half ignores human presence and an onlooker can appreciate at leisure its gay, warm colouring and plumage pattern. At other times it seldom pauses long enough among the gum leaves, which are usually larger than the bird, for one to notice more than the short stout bill, the short stocky body, the 'muslin' spots and the fiery rump. The call notes, coming untraceably from the foliage overhead, go on—to some people's annoyance— through the long hours of a sunny day and become more insistent towards sundown. Streams not too heavily bordered by eucalypts are likely spots for the 'Sleep, my baby' lullaby. Of the other half-dozen diamond birds, the Red-tipped Diamond Bird, which flits over most of the mainland, is well known because of calls, no less persistent, sounding like 'Witchy-chew' and 'Witta-witta'. It is about an inch larger than the Spotted Diamond Bird. Its white eyebrow begins as a clear yellow line near the base of the bill and on the wing is a red spot.

SPOTTED DIAMOND BIRD

NATURAL SIZE 3¼″   *Reproduced about 2/3 natural size*

MISTLETOE BIRD   *Dicæum hirundinaceum*

RECOGNITION: Aus. Crimson, black and white; diminutive. (2)

DESCRIPTION: 3½. Upper parts scintillating blue-black; throat, chest and under tail coverts rich, bold red; remaining under parts white, black line dividing lower breast; legs black; bill blackish; iris brown. *Female*, upper parts brown; tail black; under parts grey-buff; under tail coverts subdued red.

This vital midget of a bird is not rare: it inhabits both close and open woodlands; but its quick, interlacing transit through the higher foliage and its unobtrusive size often conceal it. In the tropical bush the male outbraves the butterflies in brilliance, but scarcely exceeds their spread in flight; a minute glowing scrap of life that warms the senses. The less picturesque female is often close at hand; it is engaging to see the rapid courtship chases and mounting flights with low lively chatter between the two and small, pleasing snatches of song from the cock bird. The flower-peckers are fidgets, twisting and turning and not still even when perched. The food—nectar, pollen and berries, mainly the mistletoe berry—has a delicacy appropriate to these brilliant, intensely alive bird miniatures. Some insects are taken. The birds are blamed for spreading forest mistletoes, but certainly are not the sole seeders of the parasites. The nest, sack-shaped, with a narrow side entry, formed of cobwebbed and close-woven fibres with dry flower-heads perhaps worked in, is generally low in undergrowth, but may be slung from inaccessibly high twigs. The cradle is strong, yet its dainty structure again seems in character with the builders.

MISTLETOE BIRD

NATURAL SIZE $3\frac{1}{2}''$ *Reproduced about 2/3 natural size*

GREY-BACKED SILVER-EYE   *Zosterops lateralis*

RECOGNITION: N.S.W., Vic., S.A., Tas. White spectacles; small green bird; works through foliage in flocks. (2,5)

DESCRIPTION: 4½. Crown, face, chin, lower back light green; wings green, dark grey on primaries and secondaries; white ring around eye; upper back grey; upper tail blackish-grey, margined green; upper breast grey; abdomen warm buff; under tail coverts white, tinged green; legs and bill grey; iris dark brown.

Of the Zosteropidae, the White- or Silver-Eyes, which are widely spread over Australia, the Grey-backed Silver-Eye is perhaps the most often seen, being replaced to the north and west by other forms having yellower or paler grey plumage. They are abundant, briskly flitting atomies, with a constant call, 'See-see', or 'Tseer-tseer', as they pry, probe and peer for grubs and the smaller insects, native berries and fruits among the trees and bushes. The flocks of varying numbers persist except when the pairs break off to nest, and are rather exclusive, the silver-eyes seldom mingling with other species. They rarely come to ground; if disturbed they stream jerkily to a more distant tree and continue their hunt. The busy cleaning operations throughout the year more than counterbalance damage to soft fruits when they ripen, though that may be serious. The male works up an active little song in the breeding season, which has quieter echoes in autumn; and he is a mimic of many birds. His immaculately white spectacles add a look of great intentness to all his investigations; his plumage, which can be noted at close quarters, is delicately beautiful. The West knows its Silver-Eyes as 'Greenies'. Some orchard owners appreciate the visitors as voluntary helpers. Others sullenly wipe them out.

GREY-BACKED SILVER-EYE

SCARLET ROBIN   *Petroica multicolor*

RECOGNITION: Non-tropical Aus. White disc prominent over bill; 'pillar-box' breast; black chin. (1,2)

DESCRIPTION: 5. Upper parts black, except white forehead patch, white blotch on wing and white outer tail feathers; throat and chin black, breast scarlet, abdomen white, thighs grey; legs and bill black; iris brown. *Female*, brownish-grey replaces black; suffused red on breast.

Brilliantly coloured, and with a sharply outlined neatness of plumage, the Scarlet Robin makes a 'cut-out' that contrasts with its surroundings and compels attention. A male Scarlet Robin in a bush is as obvious as a ripe fruit—indeed, he shines like a signal lamp. Pairs mostly keep together; the cock does not wholly put in the shade the female's quieter plumage: she, too, in less flamboyant fashion, is a beautiful bird. In spring and summer the white-caps keep to the higher bush and slopes; in the cold months they jaunt down to paddocks and orchards nearer sea level. The male has a cheerful trill and an energetic, sibilant alarm. During the winter robins will hunt close to a house for insects.

FLAME ROBIN   *Petroica phoenicea*

RECOGNITION: N.S.W., Vic., S.A., Tas. White forehead patch less obtrusive than Scarlet Robin's and mantle is dustier black; throat and breast fiery red. (1,2)

DESCRIPTION: 5. Upper parts greyish-black; white forehead area smaller than Scarlet Robin's; outer tail feathers show white in flying; wing coverts less white; chin blackish, throat red; abdomen whitish; legs and bill black; iris brown. *Female*, upper parts brown; breast greyish-brown, faint pinkish tinge; more subdued colouring than female Scarlet Robin.

Habits similar to Scarlet Robin's. Song more vigorous.

SCARLET ROBIN

FLAME ROBIN

NATURAL SIZE ABOUT 5″   *Reproduced about 1/2 natural size*

17

SOUTHERN YELLOW ROBIN   *Eopsaltria australis*

RECOGNITION: Eastern Aus., mainly Vic., and south-eastern S.A. Lemon-yellow breast, dark mantle; confiding, friendly. (2)

DESCRIPTION: $5\frac{1}{2}$. Breast and abdomen yellow; throat whitish-grey; upper parts blackish-grey, rump greenish-yellow; legs and bill black; iris blackish.

The Southern Yellow Robin, a forward little bird, is common on the eastern side of the continent and is well liked; in the west he gives way to robins that do not show so much of the characteristic yellow. Except in the early and closing hours of the day, he is rather silent and his near, hopeful presence to watch what may turn up in a spell of gardening work often comes as a sudden surprise. Waiting on the ground, or—a typical robin attitude—fixed aslant low down on a tree-bole, he solemnly follows the labour of the spade. At a bush picnic you may become aware of him, looking on with the intention of being a guest. The disposition to go half-way towards human company and, no doubt, the bright waistcoat give him the best of security—popularity. The yellow robin hardly produces a song, but, rather, notes that impinge on the ear. The high piping call, his chief utterance, when in cover on some dark afternoon or before going to roost, is emptily persistent and not at all blithe. Worms, insects and seeds make up his main food.

RED-CAPPED ROBIN   *Petroica goodenovii*

RECOGNITION: Aus. Slightly smaller than the Flame Robin; vivid red forehead patch. (1,2)

DESCRIPTION: $4\frac{1}{2}$. Except for forehead coloration, very similar to preceding robins; smaller area of red on breast; seasonal movements similar; song limited and less musical. *Female,* breast grey, no red tinge; ruddy to brown tint on forehead.

SOUTHERN YELLOW ROBIN

RED–CAPPED ROBIN

NATURAL SIZE ABOUT 5″   *Reproduced about 1/2 natural size*

WILLIE WAGTAIL *Rhipidura leucophrys*

RECOGNITION: Aus. except Tas. Black and white; flirts and flutters; long fan-tail swung side to side; intimate and gay. (1,5)

DESCRIPTION: 8. Upper parts, head and throat black, brownish on wing quills; well-marked white eyebrow; under parts white; legs and bill black; iris dark brown.

This trim flycatcher has danced its way into the affections of everybody. It is a 'universal favourite', because there are few areas it does not enliven. Wagtails appreciate the human being —or the cleared expanses of garden surroundings he provides; and they will nest low and visibly in a tree hard by the front door. On a bright day the little jackanapes, his contrasted plumage shining, is in continual agitation—a small bird-fountain of movement in the sunlight, singing an artless song which has been attempted in words as 'Sweet pretty creature'. Sometimes the phrase is virile, sometimes idle and languishing; on warm nights, especially when there is a moon, the lisping notes go on until the small hours. The alarm is a husky rattle. The bird was named in reminiscence of the British Pied Wagtail and 'Willie' was added as an endearing prefix. The British bird, which is less aerial, sports its tail not from side to side, but up and down. Here this well-known flycatcher dodges confidently at the noses or between the legs of grazing animals for insects, casually using their backs as an excursion platform; and he will hang hopefully round a gardener. Only during nesting is close approach not tolerated. Against birds he is courageous, buffeting crows, magpies and cuckoos, and challenging hawks.

WILLIE WAGTAIL

NATURAL SIZE 8″   *Reproduced about 1/2 natural size*

21

BROWN FLYCATCHER *Microeca fascinans*

RECOGNITION: Aus. Unobtrusive brown-grey; outer tail markedly white when flitting for insects. (1)

DESCRIPTION: 5. Upper parts brown-grey; under parts ashy; tail darker, tipped white, and outer feathers white in flight; legs and bill black; iris dark brown.

Post Boy, Jacky Winter, Spinks—half-a-dozen unofficial names suggest the friendly feeling towards this quiet, confidential, contented bird which establishes itself in orchard or garden and lives with the ambition, it seems, of keeping the zone free of flies and mosquitoes. It is a neutral-coloured bird, with conspicuous markings only when the rail is spread saliently displaying, in white, half a St Andrew cross. Regard for it springs from its amiable, unassuming personality. In the midst of its business it keeps a part eye on humans, but without distrust. With a flutter, it picks an insect from the wire or post of a fence, loops into a tree and hardly sits before again dropping to the ground. There another morsel is snatched and carried to a third perch. It has no swagger or parade, but shows a cheerful, matter-of-fact industriousness. In spring there is a song, of no great compass, but sweet and pleasing; one phrase that may be transcribed 'Peter, Peter, Peter' is responsible for another of its country names. The Brown Flycatcher shows seasonal movements, coming to lower ground and nearer the coast for the winter. The small tightly-bound nest is well concealed in tree-forks.

BROWN FLYCATCHER

NATURAL SIZE 5″   *Reproduced about 1/2 natural size*

RESTLESS FLYCATCHER   *Seisura inquieta*

RECOGNITION: Aus. Sheeny blue-black and white; tern-like hover; prolonged spinning, jingling song. (1,2)

DESCRIPTION: 8. Upper parts metallic blue-black; under parts white, including throat and chin; slight erectile crest; legs and bill black; iris dark brown. *Female*, breast faintly suffused buff.

This flycatcher is apt to be confused with the Willie Wagtail. Points of difference are that the Restless Flycatcher has no white eyebrow and his white under-plumage runs up to the bill, whereas the throat of the more common bird is black. There are more subtle differences—the Restless Flycatcher has a bluer shade in the mantle, a slimmer, more suave appearance and a more resolute bearing. Then there is the protracted hover, two or three feet clear of the ground, with the body poised almost upright. Song settles the question. Nothing is quite like the notes which have made 'Scissors-grinder' a name for the bird. They usually accompany the up-and-down, swinging hover: the widely open bill pours a sequence of whirring, skirling, spinning, threshing sounds—a knife sharpened on a steel, a machine-like racketing with altering pitch, as though the mechanism gained and lost momentum. The performance is strange, and not unpleasing. The call, given with emphasis, is a piercing 'Twee-twee-twee'. The alarm syllable is a loud squelch. The bird has an effect of decision, whether insect-catching, singing or defending territory. Bold and indifferent, it will give its curious solos and mid-air ballets close at hand in the garden. Like Willie Wagtail, the Restless is an assertive bird, but the two have a tolerance for each other and will build in adjoining areas.

RESTLESS FLYCATCHER

NATURAL SIZE 8″   *Reproduced about 1/2 natural size*

GREY FANTAIL *Rhipidura flabellifera*

RECOGNITION: Aus. Smaller, more grey than Willie Wagtail; long tail margined with white; acrobatic. (1,2)

DESCRIPTION: 6. Upper parts sooty grey; eye-streak, double bar on wing, and outer tail feathers at base, white; under parts buff; dark band across upper chest; throat white; legs dark brown; bill black; iris brown.

'Cranky Fan' displays a gusto for life, a nimble vitality and a confident front to all comers. These smaller, streakier fly-catchers have a double dose of assurance; they will chase a fly from a man's shoulder and, feverishly snapping, pursue it round his head. Few birds exert themselves more excitedly, tumble about with such determination, and find it harder to stay still. The annual work of sitting on eggs must be a trial to them. Cranky Fan rejoices in a delirium of animation if an intruder will only offer an excuse. The posturing, pirouetting and tail-fanning actions are jerky, but do not prevent the flycatchers from showing grace—the agitation is not fretful, but bursting with springiness and spirit. A twittering soft song may be thrown in with the music hall display of half a dozen winter-flocking birds. The Grey Fantails belong rather more to the bush than Willie Wagtail and the Restless Flycatcher; they visit and build in gardens less often. The nest, like Willie Wagtail's, is a cup beautifully woven, and has an extension, a projection, from the base of the bowl, rather like the pendent to an old clay tobacco pipe. Supposi-tions are that this terminal stem strengthens or balances the nest; more probably it is an expedient of camouflage.

GREY FANTAIL

NATURAL SIZE 6″   *Reproduced about 1/2 natural size*

EASTERN SPINEBILL   *Acanthorhyncus tenuirostris*

RECOGNITION: Eastern Aus., Q'ld to S.A., Tas. Long, slim down-curved bill; white expanse of throat enclosed in dark necklace. (2,5)

DESCRIPTION: 6½. Crown, nape, wings and tail, blue-black; upper back chestnut; outer tail feathers white; throat and chest white with central dull chestnut patch, encircled black from shoulder to shoulder; abdomen golden chestnut; underwing and undertail white; bill black; legs blackish; iris red.

A bird so decorative and so intricately marked is more difficult to describe than to recognize. The long decurved bill settles the identification—it looks disproportionately elongated, like the wren's tail. The strong chestnut plumage and the white throat, with its dark, contrasting surround, also quickly fix attention. The spinebill is often noticed in the garden, a visitor as gaily clad as the flowering shrubs it ransacks. It will move on the ground beneath them, obliquely probing upwards, or, on vibrating wings, make a prolonged hovering survey of the flowers before alighting to slip about the stems and twigs. Perennial salvias it loves, as butterflies love buddleias; and among woodland trees banksias are a favourite. Flight is headlong and jerky when the bird is startled, with a loud flaring of small wings; when it flits more composedly the spinebill has a string of clear, bubbling notes and a pleasant, acid little trill. In a limited south-west region of the continent, the Western Spinebill, with brighter chestnut on the throat and banding the neck, sings better still amid the jarrah, marri and the superb jungle of wild flowers in the warm bushland.

EASTERN SPINEBILL

WHITE-PLUMED HONEYEATER   *Meliphaga penicillata*

RECOGNITION: Aus. except N.T. and north Q'ld. Inspiriting, ringing 'Chick-o-wee'; restless; greenish bird, white bar on neck. (2-5)

DESCRIPTION: 6½. Upper parts greyish-brown, with suggestion of olive-green which appears clearly on wings and tail; sides of head, forehead, yellow; behind ear-coverts white plume shows as transverse neck stripe; under parts grey, with suggestion of yellow which appears clearly on breast and throat; legs light brown; bill black; iris dark brown.

'Greenie' is everybody's name in eastern Australia for this easily seen honeyeater. Usually it is the loud, repeated calls that report it first. 'Chick-o-wee!', carrying over the garden or the bush, is among the blithest of bird sounds. Clear and vibrant, with a rising lilt, it coaxes away depression, seeming to express the elation of blue skies and to salute the sunlight. As if for extra zest, the 'native canary' often launches into the air from a tree-top to broadcast and accentuate the song. The forthrightness with which it presses among the leaves and branches similarly bespeaks energy. Insects are sought as much as the pollen and nectar of flowers, and the brusque pursuit is cheerfully noisy. Other small birds are bustled out of the foliage and a kookaburra or magpie perching near greenies will not enjoy any peace. Mewing and censorious outcries convey so much concentrated disfavour that powerful birds become sick of such compliments and move on. Greenies, again, are among every community's keenest long-range look-outs, avid to give away a horizon hawk.

WHITE–PLUMED HONEYEATER

NATURAL SIZE $6\frac{1}{2}''$ *Reproduced about 1/2 natural size*

NEW HOLLAND HONEYEATER *Meliornis novae-hollandiae*

RECOGNITION: Southern Q'ld, N.S.W., Vic., S.A., south-western Aus., Tas. Streaky black and white; gold on mid-wing and tail margins; restless. (2-5)

DESCRIPTION: 7. Upper and under parts mainly black, conspicuously streaked white; white on chin, forehead, side of neck and tail tip; mid-wing gold patch obvious when perched; outer tail feathers golden; legs and decurved bill black; iris white.

This honeyeater, in its fine feathers, has self-possession; it seems as much the owner of the tended grounds of a suburban home as of the haphazard, empty scrubs of the south-west coast. With the utmost resoluteness it speeds to and fro, chattering loudly if anything disrupts its serenity and calling shrilly and emphatically—a general show of bustle and business and preoccupation with honey and insects. The restless flight and streaky, stippled plumage give the bird a slightly dishevelled look. In one garden which two pairs occupied, they confidently took over the small ornamental fountain and sported incessantly in the water, on hot days turning into balls of black and gold rags. Their loud-pitched notes, gay dress and sudden transits gave the surroundings movement and charm. This bird may be mistaken for the White-cheeked Honeyeater, which is less common and more local, and has more white about the head. Names sometimes used— White-bearded Honeyeater and Yellow-winged Honeyeater —rather add to the confusion between two black, white and gold birds of similar size; and it seems best to anglicize the official nomenclature.

NEW HOLLAND HONEYEATER

NATURAL SIZE 7″   *Reproduced about 1/2 natural size*

BELL MINER   *Manorina melanophrys*

RECOGNITION: Southern Qld to southern Vic. Olive-green. Unmistakable repetitive note metallic 'Tink!' Chubby, squinting aspect. (3, 5)

DESCRIPTION: 7. Upper parts green; under parts yellowish; black streak from gape; strong yellow patch between bill and eye; red spot behind eye; bill stout and curved, yellow; legs pink; iris brown.

This bush hobgoblin is incorrigible. Each of its tribal flocks is a clan on the war-path. The solitary utterance, fairly spat out, is the piercing 'Tink' produced by striking an orchestra triangle. Two hundred yards off, softened by distance and cover, the chime sounds delightful and remarkable. But if a colony takes over a garden, the everlasting notes are an ear-splitting bore. That is not the worst. The Bell-Bird muscular gang, of about a score upwards, labours to clear out old residents and visitors, assaulting them viciously. The defenceless are savaged. Anything less than a dangerous hawk is set upon; ravens or currawongs, for example, after enduring mob-poking and pressure and mewing and screeching rushes, move away for the sake of peace. The Bell Miner will nest in bushes against the house wall and arrogantly rate the owner if he comes out. The birds lob restlessly about their trees and peer sardonically from the branches but—against common saying—they do drop to ground, especially at the chance of a hose-bath. The oppressive little gargoyles are bark grub-hunters and seek some nectar. Having dragooned the population, they like to take over timbered rises close to creeks, within a few years (one is assured) passing on to another stronghold. For ten riotous years a contingent has firmly held a corner of my sanctuary, its sole absence being for the duration of a bush fire.

BELL MINER

EASTERN SHRIKE-TIT *Falcunculus frontatus*

RECOGNITION: Eastern and south-eastern Aus. Heavy black band across white cheeks; stumpy, thick beak; rich yellow breast. (2)

DESCRIPTION: $7\frac{1}{2}$. Head, nape and throat and broad stripe through eye to neck, black; side-face white; upper parts lively olive-green, darker on wing primaries and tail; breast and abdomen strong yellow; undertail grey; crown feathers frequently bristle into short crest; legs dark brown; bill and iris black.

'Bark-Tit' is a good country name for this robust, prying bird. If, in the bush, small lumps, shreds and splinters come sifting down, you may expect to see the shrike-tit, vividly yellow among the leaves, moving to the next patch of trunk he intends to wrench and hammer. He does his best to make good the absence of woodpeckers in Australia; on a quiet day you can hear, some way off, the stab and drive of his pick-lock beak and his ruthless ripping away of covering for moth, grub or beetle. The shrike-tit is a full-time tree and orchard surgeon, ever on his round. When busy, he stands no interfering nonsense. He often visits gardens: in one, a house sparrow, which arrived chirring and officious, was knocked headlong by the heavy, specialized beak, used as fiercely as a Roman short-sword. In autumn and winter small parties of Eastern Shrike-Tits work together with much *sotto voce* babble, including a buzzing comb-and-paper noise. When the crest is expanded the very boldly marked black and white head, set on a muscular neck, looks especially large, as among the woodpeckers. The shrike-tit again resembles a woodpecker in its looping, easy flight from tree to tree. The Western Shrike-Tit is more uniformly green on the upper parts.

EASTERN SHRIKE–TIT

WHITE-THROATED TREE-CREEPER *Climacteris leucophaea*

RECOGNITION: Eastern Aus. south of the Tropic of Capricorn, S.A. Dingy bird, white bib; spiralling up tree trunks. (2)

DESCRIPTION: 6½. Cap black; back dull brown, green trace about shoulder; lighter brown on wing; wing coverts and flanks speckled lighter; chin and throat white; abdomen whitish; legs blackish; bill and iris, dark brown. *Female*, orange spot between ear and neck. *Young*, upper tail coverts rufous brown.

In the gloom of trees only the white of chin and throat betrays this preoccupied insect hunter, looking lonely and funereal even though the female is, as a rule, not far away. The tree-creeper may come to the garden, but is more at ease in the quiet recesses of scrub or forest. One rarely catches the bird taking leisure or sees it on the ground; its hours are portioned out to a steady, methodical inspection of bark. Decayed strips and loosened shreds dissolve under quick strokes of the bill as the climber works sideways and upwards, spiralling about the trunk in a mouse-like gliding progress. When the boughs are reached, they may be hunted over, rather less closely; then the tree-creeper planes down to the base of a neighbouring gum and identical labour begins again. An audience is not welcomed. After being watched for a while, the male may throw out a series of quick, piping notes which, in the stillness of the bush, sound piercing, impatient and loud. With that protest he summons his mate to an inviolate quarter of woodland. Some forest clearings are ruled by the slightly larger Brown Tree-Creeper. He also has a high reiterated call and is constantly industrious on the ground and over fallen logs—hasty hop, pause, hurried peck and on again—as well as sidling up trees. Australia has no woodpeckers, but in default tree-creepers habitually are accorded the name.

WHITE-THROATED TREE-CREEPER

NATURAL SIZE 6½″   *Reproduced about 1/2 natural size*

WELCOME SWALLOW   *Hirundo neoxena*

RECOGNITION: Aus. Erratic flight, rapid, swooping, graceful; long, pointed wing; forked tail; twittering song. (1)

DESCRIPTION: 6. Head, back and rump blue-black; band of white spots across tail; under parts soiled white; upper chest, throat and forehead rust-red; legs horn; bill slate; iris dark brown. *Female* may show less red. *Young*, duller, stumpier tail.

The Welcome Swallow is the southern counterpart of the Barn, Eave or Chimney Swallow celebrated in northern song—'the greatest ornament a house can have', thought Richard Jefferies. Almost everywhere the flash of the Australian swallow's wing will be noticed in some month of the twelve. Though flocks leave for the warmer parts of the country after a second, or perhaps third, brood has been raised, some pairs stay in the south every winter to rough out the blasts from the Bight. In the west, as far as is known, there is no migration. The birds are continual, adroit flyers, whether on passage at ten thousand feet or frisking a fly from a grass-stem or cutting a dam surface for insects. The song is chuckling, rippling and confidential; the flight and alarm calls, 'Whit-wheet', are emphatic. The nest, marbled together with mud and stiffened with bents, may be built jointly and lined within a week. It forms a half-cup and is often placed beneath the overhang of a roof or inside a verandah. The most curious choice I have seen was under the decking of Goolwa ferry: to feed the young the parents followed each traverse of the punt. Swallows are thought to be the only birds to allow human hands to help with the nest. They were believed by old-time naturalists, to whom migration was largely unknown, to winter buried in the muddy bottom of ponds.

WELCOME SWALLOW

NATURAL SIZE 6"   *Reproduced about 1/2 natural size*

41

FAIRY MARTIN *Hylochelidon ariel*

RECOGNITION: Aus. Smaller, shorter tailed than Welcome Swallow; white on rump. (1)

DESCRIPTION: $4\frac{3}{4}$. Upper parts black, rust-coloured on head; rump and under parts soiled white; tail slightly forked; legs, bill and iris, black.

Martins are frequently called swallows, but the Fairy Martin is smaller and the plumage of the back is more faintly tinted with blue. From above the white flash of rump is distinctive; from the ground the less robust flight and less obviously forked tail are guides. In habits and food martins resemble swallows. Though their flocks are seldom large, they are more gregarious. The greatest number I have watched hawking together was in a bush-fire area when swarms of insects had been smoked out. Northward winter movements appear more regular than those of the Welcome Swallow; the martin may be less willing to put up with cold. The corresponding bird in Britain, the House Martin, builds a mud cup nest, perhaps a score rim to rim, at the angle of roof and wall. The Fairy Martin may also build in a close row. But he likes more seclusion—bridges, culverts, creek banks and cliffs are favourite sites—and the architecture is more elaborate than the House Martin's. For entrance the nest is given a spout a few inches long: whatever the original purpose, it serves nowadays to discourage the claim-jumping sparrow. In a big colony, a maze of birds will dizzily thread the arch of a bridge with insect-food for the young, marvellously avoiding collision and sweeping unerringly to the narrow bulls-eyes of their nests.

FAIRY MARTIN

NATURAL SIZE $4\frac{3}{4}''$ *Reproduced about 1/2 natural size*

DUSKY WOOD-SWALLOW *Artamus cyanopterus*

RECOGNITION: Aus. except Tas. and tropical north. Dark bird with white tail tip; glissades from perch to perch. (2)

DESCRIPTION: 7. Upper parts delicate grey-brown; wings smoky black, outlined white; tail, except central feathers, banded white; legs greyish-black; bill blue, tipped black; iris blackish.

The chase of insects by the Welcome Swallow, in comparison with the Dusky Swallow's pursuit, is jaunty, rapid and continuous—even capricious. The characteristic of the more sombre bird's flight is a slow sailing, an unwavering glide, usually not long sustained. It can move swiftly enough; but when making a round of three or four favourite perches in glades or clearings, the deliberate, smooth glide carries it from one look-out to the next. In the course of each journey, an insect disappears. The Dusky Wood-Swallow looks heavier than the Welcome Swallow: the spread of wing is broader, more triangular; and the blunt, not forked, tail, with two end-wedges of white, sets it apart. The velvet sweeps from bough to bough, while the bird keeps as silent as the trees, lend a rhythmic, ritual, slightly mysterious air. One curious name is the 'Sordid' Wood-Swallow. 'Sombre', even 'murky', might be admissible; sordid is hardly apt—the grey-tinted mantle has the delicacy of bloom on a grape. In cool weather companies of the birds, usually from fifty to seventy but even as many as two hundred, make a practice of clustering for the night on the rough bark of a tree trunk. The huddle conserves body temperature and is a trick used by some other birds here and by wrens in Britain.

DUSKY WOOD–SWALLOW

WHITE-BROWED WOOD-SWALLOW *Artamus superciliosus*

RECOGNITION: Aus., uncommon in west. Maroon breast; white line over eye; black-helmeted effect. (1,2)

DESCRIPTION: 8½. Upper parts grey-black, bluish on wings; tail tipped white; white eyebrow prominent against dark head; throat grey-black; underwing grey; breast claret; legs grey; beak blue, whitish at base, dark at tip; iris dark brown.

This species, of more presence and size than the other wood-swallows, is the most beautiful, noisy and active. The sumptuously-hued breast and streak over the eye, widening as it runs back, at once arouse notice and identify it. White-brows sometimes feed on the ground, looking for insect-food in the grass; sometimes they hawk low, gliding almost as expertly as the Dusky Wood-Swallow; and sometimes on fine evenings they chase high-flying insects, soaring and racing together or hanging hawk-like in the air, the lovely colour of the breast feathers brightened in the upshot beams of the sunset. When the birds mass together in a leafy bush or tree, their brisk 'Chip-chip-chip' may be heard before they are seen. They have many notes, guttural and mewing, and a chirring, prattling drawn-out converse like the Welcome Swallow's. They are birds of summer in the south, moving from the north usually in small flocks of a dozen or score. The inspiriting visitors haunt the fringes of a creek or a wooded paddock for some days, then vanish. These fine birds boldly allow themselves to be viewed—fortunately, for their movements are unpredictable and it may be several seasons before they pass the same way.

WHITE-BROWED
WOOD-SWALLOW

NATURAL SIZE 8½″   *Reproduced about 1/2 natural size*

GREY SHRIKE-THRUSH   *Colluricincla harmonica*

RECOGNITION: Eastern Aus., S.A., Tas. Soft greys and browns; rich, distinctive far-carrying notes. (2)

DESCRIPTION: 9½. Head, shoulders, throat, breast flanks and tail grey; back warm brown; head, throat and breast faintly seamed with black lines; lighter colouring around eye; legs and bill grey; iris black.

The Native Thrush deserves more celebrity. If there is no wide variety in his song, his is one of the magnificent bird voices, with contralto bursts of almost nightingale quality. Like the Nightingale and the English Song Thrush, the Grey Shrike-Thrush is a pattern singer. His stave opens with a sequence, four or five notes of the same pitch, with a lifting, shorter end-note. The measured opening phrase is low and mellow, but powerful; and it is sometimes given the deliberate, gushing crescendo perfected by the Nightingale. There are subsidiary whistlings, but not outstandingly good. The single call note, and warning, often sounded as the bird flies, is characteristic—a shriller, almost yelping utterance. 'Harmonious Thrush' is another name. It may be a little stilted, but it suits the bird's disposition and colouring as well as song. The plumage is a blend and soft gradation of brown and pearl greys: the grey may include bluish or mauve tints and the brown mantle deepen into chocolate. The thrush's manner is mild and peace-loving; its gentle demeanour and the large dark eyes give a suggestion of appealing intelligence. These shrike-thrushes are trustful and entirely useful. As well as other insects, they will eat caterpillar species which most birds find unpalatable, and they like the seeds of plantains and other weeds. A less admirable trait detected in a minority of thrushes is nest-robbing of eggs and fledglings.

GREY SHRIKE–THRUSH

NATURAL SIZE $9\frac{1}{2}''$ *Reproduced about 1/2 natural size*

RUFOUS WHISTLER *Pachycephala rufiventris*

RECOGNITION: Aus. White gorget, necklaced black; reddish-brown belly; loud, hurrying, silvery song. (2)

DESCRIPTION: 6¼. Upper parts grey, head darker; chin and throat white, outlined with black band; under parts chestnut-red, grey-brown under tail; legs slate; bill black; iris red-brown. *Female* and *young*, no red under.

Whether seen or heard, the Rufous Whistler plainly declares himself. The male's black-looped bib reveals him, and the rapid, pouring, silver-noted song compares with the Blackcap's in Europe, preferred by some to the Nightingale. The Rufous Whistler's phrases are not only rich, clear and profuse, but also unusually loud: the two often employed call notes— 'Ee-chong' and 'Chong-dit'—have an impulsive strength that carries a quarter of a mile. The ringing woodland choruses also include thin, pensive whistles and a minor swishing echo of the whipbird. In the eastern States, the birds move south in spring and take territory in clumps of timber; there is a recrudescence of the music before they leave in March. The singers mostly stay half-invisible among the leaves twenty or thirty feet overhead, but they are not difficult to single out. The noise of a shot or the clatter of a truck is promptly answered by a full-throated tirade. Their diet is insects. The Golden Whistler, which is less evenly spread, is more striking in appearance, with green on the back, and bright yellow plumage replacing the chestnut-red area of the Rufous Whistler. Its fine song is less emphatic, though not dissimilar.

RUFOUS WHISTLER

NATURAL SIZE $6\frac{1}{4}''$ *Reproduced about 1/2 natural size*

SONG THRUSH *Turdus musicus* Linn.

RECOGNITION: Vic., S.A. Light breast boldly marked with blackish-brown spots. Ringing song, phrases repeated. (2,5)

DESCRIPTION: 8½. Upper parts dark olive-brown; under parts whitish, tawny on breast and flanks; breast noticeably spotted; legs pale brown; bill dark brown; iris hazel.

The British Song Thrush was a good introduction to Australia for its music alone. The clear soprano may be heard throughout most of the year: on white winter mornings the throstle is sometimes the soloist of a silent world. Yet the famous song is not so sweet, so luxuriant or so confident as in the moist air of its home-land. Heat and aridity do not suit the thrush, which has settled principally in a belt of coastal country to the south, where it prefers to be near creeks. The lawns in Melbourne's parks and gardens are a stronghold where some males sing their well-defined phrases with almost native gusto. The performance is usually from a perch in plain view, and sometimes a short passage borrowed from Australian companions may be recognized. 'Tchuck!', the abrupt call note, is uttered as the bird hops over grass 'listening' for worms, slugs and insects; but the intent sideways pose of the head is for better vision, not hearing. The eye appears contemplative and staring. Snails are a delicacy for the thrush: the shell is hammered on stones or hard ground until it breaks. When startled, the bird jumps into brisk flight, with a high-pitched, rattling warning. The immigrant is not likely to be confused with the silent Australian Ground Thrush, which is more heavily mottled, has distinct black crescents covering the flanks, and keeps clear of cities.

SONG THRUSH

NATURAL SIZE $8\frac{1}{2}''$ *Reproduced about 1/2 natural size*

WHITE-FRONTED CHAT   *Ephthianura albifrons*

RECOGNITION: Southern Q'ld, N.S.W., Vic., S.A., south-western
Aus., Tas. White face in black ring encircling head
and chest. (3)

DESCRIPTION: 4½. Head and expanse of chest pure white; black
cincture back of head through mid-chest; back
soft grey, shading black on wing coverts; tail black,
tipped white; belly white; legs and bill black; iris
light brown. *Female*, no black on head; chest band
slighter, dark brown.

This little wanderer, a surprising apparition, might be wearing
a dress shirt and black waistcoat of rounded, old-fashioned
cut. 'Nun', the country name, describes the sombrely-framed
countenance and the white frontal expanse—in the midst of
which the black bill starts out like a snub nose. Black and white
plumage usually stamps a bird with a neat, fastidious air. The
Nun, however, is comical and, as if resenting the amusement
he causes, he lets out, with a nasal emphasis, the single,
rebuking sound: 'Tang!' The spiteful ring in the note is
ludicrous. Not only that, as the chat skips from bush to fence
and about the grass tussocks, he emits husky whimpers which
might be made by an infinitely small sheep. The sturdy little
body is energetically ducked and bobbed and the tail flirted.
In pairs, or winter flocks of up to about a score, the birds
roam, restless and active; nevertheless some swamps appear
to have resident pairs. Waste and rough places with low cover
and with fresh or salt water in the offing are the White-fronted
Chat's favourite flitting grounds. The female's comparatively
humdrum colouring compels the eye much less. The children's
name for Bush Chats, dictated by the metallic notes, is
'Tintack'.

54

WHITE-FRONTED CHAT

AUSTRALIAN PIPIT *Anthus australis*

RECOGNITION: Aus. Streaked brown; rises singing, then drops abruptly to ground. (1)

DESCRIPTION: 6½. Upper parts brown, back streaked darker, line over eye lighter; outer tail feathers white; under parts white, breast streaked brown and buff; legs pale brown; bill and iris brown.

The pipit nests on the ground and passes much of its time afoot, feeding and running on the turf, taking seeds and surprising insects. In colouring and habits it is a self-effacing bird. Like the European wagtails, to which it is closely related, the Australian Pipit has a trick of swinging its tail, which is moderately long, up and down. Usually found alone or in pairs, the birds when flushed evince the pipit distaste for trekking far: a nimble run, or a flight as brief as possible, takes them out of the way. Spring spurs the pipit into vivacity; then it rises with a vaulting flight to pour out an enlivening, warbling song—yet its performance is not so loud and prolonged as the Skylark's. Breaking off the music somewhat suddenly, it parachutes to the ground. The Horsfield Bush Lark, *Mirafra javanica*, is another good soaring singer, continuing its music on moonlight nights and often weaving in the phrases of other birds; in dress it is similar enough to the Australian Pipit to cause casual confusion. The bush lark appears stockier, and has a warmer colouring; its bill is heavier and more finch-like. Many birds share the ruse of drawing off trespassers by pretending an injured wing—in this 'dodge' pipits (and the chat, the preceding bird described) place a particular and rather pathetic trust.

AUSTRALIAN PIPIT

SKYLARK *Alauda arvensis*

RECOGNITION: Vic., S.A. Mounts until it appears as speck, with shrill, vehement, continuous song, and floats down singing; brown; white outer tail feathers. (1)

DESCRIPTION: 7¾. Mantle brown, streaked darker on back and head; short crest erected while running; pale buff stripe over eye; under parts buffy white, streaked and spotted; legs red-brown; bill black, lower mandible brown; iris light brown.

In open country in the cooler regions—pasture, cleared uplands or coastal marsh—and in almost any weather except chill rain, the Skylark may rise on pointed, quivering wings and, once clear of the grass, begin the rapid, vibrant, famous song that streams on the air until the bird has risen many hundreds of feet and hangs, a pin-point of music, in the blue. Holding to the crest of the almost vertical climb with whirring wings, the lark carols on for a time, then wheels and slowly gives height, singing still, but with less vigour and sometimes in altered key. The music is broken off about a hundred feet overhead and the descent is completed in a sudden drop. Bursts of the same song are heard when the bird is on the ground, or perched on post or wire. It is the exaltation and duration, and the signal way in which the song is delivered, rather than quality and diversity—though the best lark voices have a silvery ring—which give the performance its renown. The Skylark is firmly domiciled in south-eastern Australia, but is rare in comparison with its numbers in Britain and Europe where it is a useful insectivorous and seed-eating bird. A cheerful, chirruping note is both alarm and call.

SKYLARK

RED-BROWED FINCH   *Aegintha temporalis*

RECOGNITION: Eastern Aus. from north of Q'ld to S.A. Red rump, beak and sides of head. (1)

DESCRIPTION: $4\frac{1}{2}$. Red band runs over eye from slightly lighter red beak; upper parts olivaceous brown, crown greyer, rump and upper tail coverts red; under parts lighter than mantle; legs flesh-colour; iris red-brown. *Young*, no red.

Hunting about for seeds, this brightly patched little finch is met along the roadside, in pastures and gardens, in the hedgerow and on the outskirts of sparse woodlands. When disturbed it hurries for cover on rather ineffectually whirring wings and with the anxious twitterings that are its only notes. But soon it will creep back to resume the unobtrusive, diligent search. The birds like to stay in company: when nesting is done parents and young form small parties working over bushes and, almost invisibly, through long grass. As they hop on the ground, the finches seem sober mites; but when they fly, uttering their modest call signals, the red markings at tail and head light them up. On a sunny day, suspended in a blur of wings in front of a bush that is being studied for insects and seeds, the 'Fire-tail' is seen at his bravest, and justifies a commonly used name. Another common name is 'Wax-bill'. The appeal of some birds that shun notice and seem to ask only to be permitted to pursue their small scheme of life is difficult to define; but these finches possess it. Formerly they were heavily trapped for aviaries; now their food on farm land and road verges may be heavily spray-poisoned and flocks are thinner than of old.

RED–BROWED FINCH

NATURAL SIZE $4\frac{1}{2}''$ *Reproduced about 2/3 natural size*

ZEBRA FINCH *Taeniopygia castanotis*

RECOGNITION: Aus. except Tas. Chestnut bill and cheeks; breast striped transversely black and grey. (1)

DESCRIPTION: 4. Upper parts ash-brown, greyer neck and head; cheeks chestnut; behind bill, white bar between black lines; rump white; tail coverts black, broadly barred white; chest grey, with narrow black bars and black band; flanks chestnut, with white spots; belly and undertail white; legs and bill orange; iris red.

These stocky, very barred-looking birds are unmistakable, although the female lacks the extensive chestnut 'ear'. The complex colour pattern is remarkable. In the greenery of the south the bird looks almost exotic and foreign: only in the hot northern areas are big flocks commonplace. Around water-holes during dry spells the chequered finches will flit in multitudes, careless of man. At one drinking place in the Northern Territory I saw more than a thousand gathered together; when approached they moved, with a swarming whirr of small wings, to trees only a few yards off. Even when not driven by thirst or hunger, the Zebra Finch appears trustful: it will come near homesteads, roaming among the vegetation and over the ground for seeds. These visitors to the rickyard or garden are likely to be in small numbers. In the hedges the finches sometimes perch with sparrows; against their daintily and delicately defined plumage 'Phillip' looks deplorably drab and poor. Zebra flocks are less often met along the coasts. It has a soft trilling phrase, musical when taken up and magnified by a large flock and to keep a moving company in touch a low double-syllabled call is maintained.

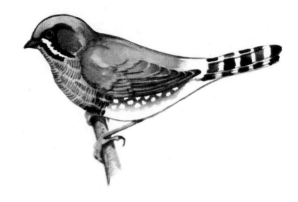

ZEBRA FINCH

NATURAL SIZE 4″   *Reproduced about 2/3 natural size*

GREENFINCH   *Chloris chloris*

RECOGNITION: Vic., southern N.S.W., S.A. Yellowish-green;
gold-margined wing and gold base to tail; musical
twittering in flight. (1,5)

DESCRIPTION: 6. Summer plumage yellow-green, winter plumage
brown-green; wings and tail-tip shaded dark grey
to blackish-brown; bright yellow wing edge and
base of tail; legs flesh-brown; bill flesh-coloured,
darker at tip; iris light brown. *Female*, browner, less
yellow.

Victoria, with its 'English' climate, is the main territory of the
Green Linnet. The drawling 'dwe-e-r', interspersed with a
soft, melodious, twittering chain of notes, is a sound that fills
the European migrant with sudden memory of summer
afternoons at home. The rather monotonous main call is
uttered from a perch; the lilting song is heard either in the
course of the undulating flight from place to place, alternating
spurts and glides with wings closed, or during hovering
excursions around the tree in which the finches are nesting.
The flocks, seldom very numerous here, hunt usefully for
seeds; the gentle quality of voice and quiet manners lead one
to welcome the birds as unsuspicious, amiable, inoffensive
visitors to the farm or garden. In the summer season these
'greenies' of the north hold their place with many of the more
dashing native birds—the flash of the wing, with the tail
picking up the golden glint, is striking. This attractive
wanderer comes to city reserves and public gardens and can
be coaxed to within a foot or two by a scatter of seeds. The
Greenfinch has not multiplied with the hardihood of the
introduced goldfinch, but pairs and occasional limited flocks
have brought an asset to Sydney, Melbourne and Adelaide.

GREENFINCH

NATURAL SIZE 6″   Reproduced about 1/2 natural size

GOLDFINCH *Carduelis carduelis*

RECOGNITION: Non-tropical Aus. Red mask surrounded by white and black; broad gold band on wing. (1)

DESCRIPTION: 5. Bands of crimson, black and white contrast on face and head; back grey-brown, except for small white patch on neck; wings black, crossed with bright gold band; tail black, tipped and spotted white; undertail and belly white; flanks brown; legs flesh tint; bill pink and white; iris brown. *Young*, streaky grey-brown, no head colours.

'Charm of goldfinches', the old collective noun for a flock, implies how winning these birds are. Bright as a Guardsman in colour, with a song clear and liquid; gay, vaulting flight and vivacious postures when ransacking weeds, this is an alluring finch. In Britain the sweet song and gay plumage were the undoing of the Goldfinch until the law forbade both its imprisonment in cages and the use of its feathers for women's titivation. A flock of ten thousand is mentioned in Cobbett's *Rural Rides*, written in about 1830. Sixty years later the Goldfinch had almost gone from many English counties. Even now the birds are commoner in Australia than in their original breeding places. As though bleached by the Australian sun, the colouring of the back appears to be greyer than in Europe. 'Thistle-finch' was urged by Macgillivray as a name, that weed being first favourite of the many the Goldfinch checks. It frequents waste, untilled land—and the untidy portion of the garden—rather than paddock and woodland. Flocks move with a dancing motion and with a rippling, tinkling, musical chorus. In spring the diet is largely transferred to insects.

GOLDFINCH

STARLING *Sturnus vulgaris*

RECOGNITION: Aus. except tropics and western Aus. Forages on ground in company; manoeuvres in dense flocks in the air; wheezing jumbled notes. (1)

DESCRIPTION: 8½. Plumage blackish, metallic-hued, glistening purple, blue, and green; closely spotted, browner in appearance after autumn moult, when feathers are tipped buff and white; legs brown or pinkish; bill brown to yellow; iris brown. *Female* rather duller. *Young*, light brown, spotted later.

Some naturalists think the Starling the world's most numerous bird. From Europe it has pushed its legions through Asia and Africa; in Australia it was enlisted as a warrior against cut-worms, grasshoppers, cockroaches and other nuisances. The rise in numbers has posed the question whether the bird now does as much harm as good; but investigations suggest that the insect slaughter more than pays for the fruit, grain and berries eaten. Self-assertive, sociable, talkative, seeming always in a hurry, the Starling lives at the pitch of his energy. He borrows other species' calls and mocks or mimics noises like the click of a gate or the ting of a shop bell. On frosty mornings on the roof-ridge, his wings shiver not with cold, but with his effort to defy the chill air with a whole opera of whistling, smacking, chuckling, comical sounds. The massed evening flights are a spectacle, the flocks thick as dust-clouds against the sunset. Strong, sharp beats of the triangular wings alternate with long glides. On the ground the feeding flock waddles forward purposefully. The alarm, a half-hiss, half-rasp, is like the swearing of a cat. People who regard birds with only a vacant eye profess to dislike starlings—but can one dislike a character so bustling and droll?

STARLING

NATURAL SIZE $8\frac{1}{2}''$ *Reproduced about* 1/2 *natural size*

FORK-TAILED SWIFT *Micropus pacificus*

RECOGNITION: Aus. Flickering, tapered wings; racing dark crescent in sky. (1)

DESCRIPTION: 7. Upper parts dingy brown, rump white; under parts brown, throat white; tail deeply forked; legs, bill and iris black.

SPINE-TAILED SWIFT *Hirundapus caudacutus*

RECOGNITION: Similar to Fork-tailed Swift; very rare in W.A.

DESCRIPTION: 8. Back brown, head, wings and tail darker, glossed green; belly brown, throat and breast white; forehead soiled white; under tail coverts white, tailfeather shafts spiny, projecting; legs, bill and iris dark brown.

In spring and summer, especially in disturbed weather, a dark sickle silhouette is seen in the sky; the long sharp wings flicker, then are held in a racing glide or make an almost vertical climb. The bird will be one of the two flashing visitors from Asia. The Spine- or Needle-tailed Swift is probably the fastest flyer in the world; its cruising speed may be more than 150 miles an hour. 'Thunder bird' is a common name for it; in England the storm-heralding swift is known as the 'Devil bird'. So aerial are swifts that it is believed they may sleep on the wing. They cannot walk and do not trust, except for clinging to raised surfaces, their short, weak legs. It is suspected (my observations inclining to support the theory) that the wings can be beaten alternately or independently, against the canons of normal flight. The swift's altitude follows its larder of small flying beetles and other insects. Flocks—sometimes the birds form big, swirling companies—have been found feeding at six thousand feet; alternatively, with no more than a clearance of inches, they may streak over the ground surface dodging obstacles by a hair—or feather.

FORK–TAILED
SWIFT

SPINE–TAILED
SWIFT

NATURAL SIZE ABOUT 8"   *Reproduced about 1/4 natural size*

SACRED KINGFISHER *Halcyon sanctus*

RECOGNITION: Aus. except Tas. Green-blue; shrill, impatient 'Ki-ki-ki-ki'. (2)

DESCRIPTION: 8. Upper parts greenish-blue; under parts buff white; nape whitish with black collar; legs brown; bill black; iris brown.

At the summit of a tree a stumpy bird with a stout, long bill, persistently calling a clear, liquid, rather protesting note—that is the typical way in which the Sacred Kingfisher is seen and heard. The calls are unlikely in the south country until October for the birds range north in the colder months, many flying on to the islands. This small kingfisher, although normally near rivers and creeks, may show himself anywhere except in heavy forest and actual desert areas; fairly open woodland is a likely neighbourhood. After the habit of most members of their family the birds sometimes appear to aim at small fish, but the dashes to the surface of the water may be for insects only. Most of the provender is sought on land, the watcher from his look-out bough planing down to take lizards, frogs and like small prey. The Sacred Kingfisher, despite his aloof name, is quite approachable. He is a striking bird when sunlight touches the green and blue-shot plumage of wings and back. The keen, querulous summons often wafts from the creek-side through the summer darkness. Towards the end of the season before departure northward, the brood being complete, the whole family holiday by a dam or secluded water and the young are shown how to respond to every invitation on the surface.

SACRED KINGFISHÉR

NATURAL SIZE 8″   *Reproduced about 1/2 natural size*

RAINBOW BIRD *Merops ornatus*

RECOGNITION: Aus. except Tas. Like iridescent swallow, with two projecting thin feathers mid-tail. (2)

DESCRIPTION: 9. Wings green, quills bronze, tipped black; tail black, two greenish middle feathers projecting some two inches as spines; upper tail coverts and lower back light blue; mantle and forehead green; nape bronze; chin yellow-orange; throat and streak through eye, black; breast green, shading blue on abdomen; under tail coverts light blue; underwing rust-rose; legs pinky grey; bill black, long, down-curved; iris red.

This slim bird, of swallow-like aspect and flight, is elusive in colour as the rainbow after which it is called; it is a brilliancy, a moving point on which the light plays in splendour—it is perhaps Australia's loveliest bird. The wings gliding overhead have a transparency, as if in the veins and the vans of this creature tropical sunlight flowed. Happily, Australia's only bee-eater is common, and neither secretive nor shy. Journeying south from the islands and the north of the continent each spring, the birds spread almost as far as the southern coast, although over the last fifty miles or more they are rare. Small parties balance on overhead wires at roadsides, announcing their arrival with vigorous, shrill, purring calls, darting off for insects and returning in flycatcher fashion. The bee-eater will snap up hive bees and heavily punish blowflies and trouble-some flying insects. This gorgeous migrant may tunnel nearly a yard into the ground to open a nesting chamber. Road-bank sites are appreciated, but not road-sealing, for the Rainbow Bird enjoys his dust-bath. He lingers about regions not thickly covered, but patched by trees and bushes.

RAINBOW BIRD

NATURAL SIZE 9″   *Reproduced about 1/2 natural size*

COMMON SANDPIPER   *Tringa hypoleuca*

RECOGNITION: Aus. Active, nods head and jerks tail up and down; cuts over water with stiff downward wing-beats. (3,4)

DESCRIPTION: 8. Upper parts greenish-brown, dark margins and centres to mantle feathers; secondaries edged white, forming bar in flight; outer tail feathers and faint line over eye, white; breast ashy-brown, streaked darker; rest of under parts white; legs greenish-grey; bill brown; iris dark brown.

World wanderers—for the Common Sandpipers breed in Europe and northern Asia—numbers of these birds pass about half the year in Australia. They feed exactly along the water-line of sandy and rocky shores, rivers, irrigation channels and farm dams, picking insects and their larvae, sand-hoppers and freshwater organisms from the moist margin of ground. Small parties are frequently interspersed with other waders; with the short tail jigging and the head incessantly nodding, they look alert and occupied. When approached they take to swift flight, the wings seeming scarcely to be brought above the level of the back and being moved with a curiously wooden, strong down-beat. The course usually carries the birds through a semi-circle to re-land on the water's edge some distance off. The bird's wayward, skimming flight and straight slender bill have earned it the nickname of 'Summer Snipe' in Britain. These graceful waders can swim and dive, but prefer to use their active, twinkling legs. The piping 'Dee-dee-dee' call when sandpipers have been scared, and the liquid trilling and whistling in the nesting season, are among the most musical waterside notes.

COMMON SANDPIPER

BLACK-FRONTED DOTTEREL *Charadrius melanops*

RECOGNITION: Aus. Black band around breast; chestnut shoulder patch; white line over eye and encircling nape. (3)

DESCRIPTION: 6. Upper parts mottled ash-brown, shoulder chestnut, whitish line above black wing-quills; hind-neck white, extending forward as line over eye; forehead black; throat and abdomen white, cut by broad black chest band; legs reddish; bill coral, black tipped; iris brown, ringed red.

This little wader, charming in grace and poise, is common at the edge of inland pools and swamps, but is rarely seen near salt water. The plumage, daintily black, white and brown, sometimes wants the full chest band in immature birds. 'Trips' is the collective noun for dotterel parties in Britain— deriving from the rapid, twinkling gait as the waders chase insects or search mud for worms and small molluscs; they run a short distance and pitch forward to take the food. In the midst of the sprint, they often stretch the wings above the back. The wing beats are sharp and powerful; on the ground they set off running as abruptly as they halt. The plumage colours of dotterel species stand out brightly in illustration, but when feeding along the watery margins their small forms are not conspicuous. The nest hollows, containing up to half a dozen eggs—grey-white with brown or reddish signatures —are carbon copies of the ground in which they have been excavated. They trick the eye; and the chicks as they 'freeze' seem to blur into nothing.

BLACK-FRONTED DOTTEREL

DOUBLE-BANDED DOTTEREL   *Charadrius bicinctus*

RECOGNITION: Aus. except north-west. Upper black band on breast and lower, broader, chestnut band separated by white band.

DESCRIPTION: 7. Upper parts brown; forehead white; black streak through eye from beak; banded under parts white; legs greenish; bill black; iris dark brown.

Along the shore-line this handsome, active dotterel is a winter visitor from New Zealand and frequently joins other waders in the hunt for small crustacea and insects. The call note is an impatient whistle. Immature birds lack, or only partly show, the under-bands, which fade or may become imperfect in the adults' winter dress. By March many of these reliable migrants have arrived for a stay of about six months. Companies that have newly touched down usually are tired, less than alert, and quickly re-settle if scared into taking wing. A few Double-Banded Dotterels are reported to have remained throughout the year.

DOUBLE-BANDED DOTTEREL

LITTLE GREBE   *Podiceps ruficollis*

RECOGNITION: Aus. Round, lively, toy-like water bird; dark above, white under. (3)

DESCRIPTION: 9½. Upper parts, chin and throat black to grey; under parts sheeny white; light patch below eye; slight white wing bar; legs green; bill black; iris amber. *Winter*, head fawn to brown.

That perfectly specialized urchin, the dabchick, with blunt rump and no tail, swims low but is as buoyant as a cork. He is scarcely ever out of fresh water, although occasionally reported along the coast. Submerged, the Little Grebe remains just as mobile; the wings are held in tightly, the feet oared sideways in jerky pursuit of tadpoles, yabbies and fish. The catch is sometimes impressively large in proportion to the bird's throat. This diver may stay down for a quarter of a minute or longer and, if at all suspicious, will surface with no more than the bill visible. Often the return is cannily made behind the overhanging cover of the bank. Should a bird be surprised at the edge of water, a hurried flutter takes him to mid-stream or pond, to vanish where he lights. He dives untiringly, ordinarily leaving little trace, yet sometimes fairly kicks himself under. The young swim and dive as soon as they feel water; they mount their parents' backs in the fashion of crested grebe broods. The 'children' may be left comically floating when their elders go below, and they hurry to scramble back on board as soon as their raft reappears. It is also on a raft that they have been reared. The nest is an amply-sized water weed platform, the parents restoring weakness or decay by fresh collections of greenery.

LITTLE GREBE

BUDGERIGAR *Melopsittacus undulatus*

RECOGNITION: Aus. except Tas. Small, green, yellow wings much barred black; dense flocks. (1)

DESCRIPTION: 8. Head, nape and wing coverts finely barred yellow and black; back and under parts rich green; throat yellow, spotted black; crown and blue-spotted cheek yellow; legs grey to light brown; beak grey; iris variable.

Minor parties of this small quick parrot come south in the winter, but in the Centre—the Budgerigar is mostly an inland resident—immense, glittering flocks rise from the levels with a tremendous drumming of wings and seething of voices. With rushing, arrowy flight they strike for a near tree; should it be one of those skeletons that are morbidly common on the desert plain, in a twinkling the bare limbs appear mossed over with brilliant verdure. The Budgerigar is loquacious: while looking for grass seeds or sitting in a tree, it prattles, chuckles and warbles with sociable energy. Demonstrative, affectionate manners have landed it in innumerable cages throughout the world as the 'Love bird'. Breeders have succeeded by selection in transforming the green feathers to sundry blues and yellows, and birds near these tints have been picked out in wild flocks. Tree-holes afford nesting places in months much determined by the weather; half a dozen white eggs may be laid. If a compulsion seizes the flock to move, the young are left. Captive Budgerigars may be coaxed to talk well; one may quickly become glib, another not.

BUDGERIGAR

LARGE BIRDS

Birds of ten inches or more from bill tip to end of tail feathers. Birds in this section are reproduced generally either to one-quarter or one-eighth natural size, but the considerable range of sizes in this category has made necessary more variation in reduction sizes. The natural size and the reduction of each bird are given below each illustration.

SUPERB LYRE-BIRD   *Menura novae-hollandiae*

RECOGNITION: S.E. Qld to eastern Vic.; central Tas. Magnificent ringing song and master-mimic; pheasant-like bird with 'peacock' display.

DESCRIPTION: 27. Upper parts brown, paler under; head black; cheeks whitish; tail outer feathers dark, mid-pair brown, filamentaries under silver-white; legs and bill black; iris brown. *Female*, lacks decorative tail.

From my notebook at first acquaintance: 'Extraordinary power, scales down other birds to status of ballad singers'. In beauty of display the Lyre-bird has rivals, but the commanding voice makes a forest into an opera house and cannot be matched for clear force and dramatic quality. Both male and female sing, mainly during May to September mating. The nest's bulky wigwam is constructed during winter, when damp litter can be sifted for 'hoppers', worms and grubs. To vary their private repertoire, Lyre-birds duplicate with condescending ease the phrases and notes of any bird and mimic mechanical and human noises. When the 'star' skips to one of the low mounds built as a stage, there may be, besides the imposing song, ceremonious dancing and swaying and the spectacular expansion of tail which—pulled like a canopy above the performer's head—transforms the reticently attired body into a veiled, silvered, mysterious symbol of a bird. Furtive in their mountain scrubs and wooded gullies, Lyre-birds have grown used to witnesses in Sherbrooke Forest, near Melbourne. The Prince Albert Lyre-bird, *M. alberta*, of S.E. Queensland and N.E. New South Wales, is slightly smaller, warmer in colouring and sings as richly, although he erects a less distinguished tail.

SUPERB LYRE-BIRD

GREY BUTCHER-BIRD   *Cracticus torquatus*

RECOGNITION: Aus. except upper portions of N.T. and W.A. Stocky, drab, white collar; flying, rump and tail fringe white; crochet-hook bill; spirited caroller.

DESCRIPTION: 11. Back grey; head, cheeks, tail black; sides of neck, rump, terminal tail band and variable wing patch white; under parts light grey; strong bill blue-grey; but black near hooked tip; legs blackish; iris brown-black.

Like a stern officer of the watch the shrike makes his rounds, an overbearing and resented presence. He arrives quietly but spurns concealment, perching in view, rocking now and then to ease his balance, 'like a cop on a New York corner', said an American guest. The domineering figure's eyes, if not prominent, are busy and the head inquisitively turns. A glance down, a precise drop and a grass-hopper has gone. The sentinel remounts, gauges the approach of a large flying insect, sallies out and returns to dismember the prey, wedged fast beneath one foot. The flight ordinarily looks heavy, but in the capturing dash there is quick purpose. Weightier victims—lizards, mice, young birds—are spitted on sturdy thorns, or a barbed wire spike will do; and among bristly bushes one may meet with the dead, impaled in the shrike's larder. Butcher-birds set aside the theory that song is a vernal 'Keep Out' notice; autumn is their finest hour for fluting, warbling and whistling. The performance is loud, mellow and rich—unstudied, impulsive music. The handsome Pied Butcher-bird, a stranger to the country's southern sector, has the name 'Organ bird'; its voice truly peals.

GREY BUTCHER-BIRD

BLACK-BACKED MAGPIE *Gymnorhina tibicen*

RECOGNITION: Aus. except southern Vic. and south-western Aus. Like parti-coloured crow; pealing, melodious chorus. (1,2)

DESCRIPTION: 15. Black, except white areas on hind neck, lower back, tail and wing; legs black; bill white, tipped black; iris brown.

The wavering, husky chime of the magpie is one of the cherished sounds of the countryside. Three closely related species, the Black-backed, the White-backed (those illustrated opposite) and the Western Magpie, more or less cover the continent between them; they have the same habits and jumbled carols and differ only in the shading of their bold and attractive dress. The birds, which are shrikes and resemble the British magpie only in coloration, form small clans; five to ten is the usual number. They claim possessively one or two paddocks, a stretch of hillside or a patch of timber, and maintain an unswerving control. While non-competitive residents are grudgingly tolerated, larger visitors—hawk, parrot or inoffensive heron—are assailed with a pandemonium of unbridled resentment. If two magpie areas are adjacent, the occupants will unite and fly together with hoarse music in graceful evening play. But vicious fights may start between representatives of the factions and greatly excite the others. After the fray the birds stand glumly defiant, with the colonies hunched in a huffy ring; presently all return to the accustomed beats. These truculent aerial watch-dogs earn their keep about a farm by dealing with many pests in pastures and cultivated ground.

BLACK-BACKED
MAGPIE

WHITE-BACKED
MAGPIE

NATURAL SIZE 15"-17"   *Reproduced about 1/5 natural size*

PIED CURRAWONG *Strepera graculina*

RECOGNITION: Eastern Aus. Black; white wing patches flying; mellow, echoing call. (1,2)

DESCRIPTION: 18. Black, except for white on wing coverts, upper and lower tail coverts and tail tip; legs and bill grey; iris yellow.

Over a large area of Australia the melodious, wafting Pied Currawong's call is one of the best-known bird voices. The name is a rendering of the cry—a harmonious tenor, or alto, resounding in bush and gully. The bird's fruity double whistle is the first greeting heard by many country risers in frosty dawns: there is a rouse, a summons, an excitation in it. Like jackdaws in Europe, the birds perch on the chimney-rim with a 'What's for breakfast?' air and seem to look with approval on the town's awakening bustle. As Australia becomes more populous they may further lose their reserve towards man; they might insinuate themselves as town daws. Friendliness may not be returned everywhere, for while the Pied Currawong helps in the war on farming pests, he gives the fruit grower some concern and shares the crow-habit of nest-raiding. Numbers vary throughout a district in the course of the year. Floods cause extensive migrations: one wet winter on the Murray brought heavy flocks almost to the south Victorian coast, to regions normally peopled by Grey Currawongs. The sly and convivial Pie is amusing to have as a garden guest, but expensive—two or three visits by a flock and from trees and shrubs all the bright berries will have vanished. Related forms, similar in habits, extend the distribution to Tasmania ('Black Jay'), South Australia, and Western Australia ('Squeaker')

PIED CURRAWONG

NATURAL SIZE 18″   *Reproduced about 1/4 natural size*

GREY CURRAWONG   *Strepera versicolor*

RECOGNITION: Eastern, southern and south-western Aus. Bulky, blundering; high-pitched ringing whistle. (1,2)

DESCRIPTION: 19. Dingy grey, wings darker; white wing patches shown flying; tail under and tip white; legs and bill grey; iris amber.

The Grey Currawongs appear larger and more gaunt than a raven or crow; they are commanding birds, but give an impression of clumsiness. Less aerial than the corvines, they move at no great height between tree belts, in summer watchfully conducting the young from cover to cover. They often land with a scramble on stems and branches not stout enough for a durable perch: other birds are disposed to leave, and the big fellow with the heavy beak steadies his balance and looks about with distrustful eyes. Grey Currawongs patiently turn over bark and leaves on the ground to surprise spiders, beetles and other morsels; it may be an hour before a bird relinquishes examination of a fallen, rotting trunk. The soprano cries uttered on the wing are rather ludicrous for a bird of such bulk and power. The notes have a pencil-on-a-slate squeakiness, but also catch something of the ringing character of the Pied Currawong's call. 'Rain bird' is a country name: the clamour is more frequent in winter months. The Pied Currawong's dash is apiece with the handsome attire. Beside him the Grey is an ordinarily clad and furtive-mannered fellow. Both are birds of forest landscapes but nudge into urban surroundings during winter.

GREY CURRAWONG

NATURAL SIZE 19″   *Reproduced about 1/4 natural size*

RAVEN   *Corvus coronoides*

RECOGNITION: Eastern Aus. to Tropic of Capricorn, southern Aus., Tas. Long-drawn, wavering 'Carr'; deeper clarion 'Gwarr-gwar'. (1,2,4)

DESCRIPTION: 20. Plumage black, glints of purple; elongated throat feathers; legs and bill black; iris white. *Young*, iris brown.

CROW   *Corvus cecilae*

RECOGNITION: N.T., Cent., Q'ld, northern N.S.W., S.A. and W.A. Shorter, more tenor note than the Raven. (1,2)

DESCRIPTION: 20. Scarcely distinguishable in field from Raven; throat hackles shorter.

These birds, typical corvines, are so much alike that where the ranges overlap difference in voice is the best evidence of identity. Except when breeding each species is gregarious; small parties, 'black crosses in the wind', make familiar sky pictures; the birds feed together and combine at any point that calls for joint interest or action. Ordinarily the congregations number about a score, but in the open miles of the far north and centre, the Crow (and his miniature, the Little Crow) flies in hosts that blacken the sky. For the Raven's depredations at lambing time the Crow is often wrongly denounced. The all-inclusive diet of the birds disposes of carrion and hordes of insects; the blowfly plague would be much worse without the scavengers. The nests, probably well up in a tree-fork, are less obvious than one would expect from their bulkiness, and the parents leave with silent circumspection. Raven and Crow come of one of the most keenly intelligent orders and exact respect and half-regard by their observant prudence, the sly, sardonic basis of their behaviour and their undefeated long guerilla with man.

RAVEN

CROW

NATURAL SIZE 20"   *Reproduced about 1/7 natural size*

99

WHITE-WINGED CHOUGH *Corcorax melanorhamphus*

RECOGNITION: Q'ld, N.S.W., Vic., S.A. 'Crow' with marked white wing-patch in flight. (2).

DESCRIPTION: 16. All black; white roundels not visible when wings at rest; iris clear red.

Small congregations of these crows move shoulder to shoulder in the bush or under road-side trees and copses, turning over the earth and fallen leaves with energy, flinging twigs and litter into the air, and finding matter for much conversation— an exchange of scolding, almost hissing sounds. Under the shadowy trees they are a sombre crew, only the tail showing much gloss and an occasional watchful gleam starting from the red eyes. They have the crow's typical rolling walk, and run with swift consternation if disturbed, giving the alarm by an ill-tempered, challenging churring. By contrast, the call-note is a flat, low whistle, with no heart in it. Only when the choughs relax their plumage to preen, or when flying, is their large white wing-patch displayed: then is it clear at any distance. A good light shows the radiation of the main quills, giving the wing a veined, semi-transparent effect, like a white butterfly's. The chough's flight is tossing and buoyant, not so steady and purposeful as the raven's or crow's, and the beak is curved and more slender and light in structure. It is not evident why the birds sometimes are shot. Their food is principally insects and larvae plus seeds and berries and their social habits are interesting. They display teamwork in nest-making and while they imitate the corvine habit of repairing old nests to impressive size, are among the only two or three Australian bird-potters that fashion a mud bowl.

WHITE–WINGED CHOUGH

NATURAL SIZE 16″   *Reproduced about 1/4 natural size*

MAGPIE LARK *Grallina cyanoleuca*

RECOGNITION: Aus., occasionally Tas. Mainly black above, white under; roughly resembles more delicate, slender magpie. (1,2)

DESCRIPTION: 12. Upper parts, crown, nape, back, wings and lower tail, black; side of neck, shoulder, tail coverts, tail tip, broad streak over, and area below and behind eye, white; under parts, throat, breast, black; abdomen, flanks, under tail coverts, white; legs black; bill whitish; iris pale yellow. *Female*, throat and forehead white.

The burly magpie looks masculine; the pert Magpie Lark has a slim and feminine aspect, an appearance of being consciously well turned-out in a chequered habit. The gait is a little mincing; the wings and tail may be petulantly flirted and the voice is shrill and excited; but for a bird so trim in outline, gait and most movements, the flight seems arduous and lagging. The slender and fastidious looks are rather misleading. The Pee-wee is vigorous and unusually widespread. It shows a determined sense of territory and no bashfulness towards trespassers near the nest. The keening calls, 'Pee-wee', 'Pee-o-wit', or 'Pee-oo-wit tee hee', are given in fervid bouts, drowning opposition voices. Pairs call in deliberate unison. One of the two determinedly tries to succeed in singing 'seconds'. While there are many examples of birds crying in loose chorus or against each other, there can be few such practised duettists. The harmonic effect is like the double-stopping of a violin. An often-used name for the bird, 'Mudlark', derives from the nest which is composed of mud reinforced by grasses—clearly not a fortress against all weathers, since heavy spring deluges may partly dissolve the structure in its supporting tree-fork.

MAGPIE LARK

NATURAL SIZE 12″   *Reproduced about 1/4 natural size*

BLACK-FACED CUCKOO-SHRIKE *Coracina novae-hollandiae*

RECOGNITION: Aus. Pale grey; mostly amid tree-tops; clear fluting calls and churring notes. (2)

DESCRIPTION: 13. Ashen grey; throat area, cheeks, forehead, wing quills and lower tail, black; belly, undertail and tip white; legs and bill black; iris dark brown. *Young*, head greyer, black line through eye and cheek.

It seems surprising that this large, beautiful and fairly common cuckoo-shrike is not more admired. The ghostly grey is a courtly dress flaunted among the leaves or against the sky and the bird might be obsessed by neatness from the typical movement which gives the name 'Shufflewing'. After alighting, the cuckoo-shrike lifts and alternately re-folds its wings, as automatically as a woman smooths her skirt on sitting down. The flight is masterful and easy: a looping, cruising passage from one patch of woodland to the next, or drifting glides and circlings that make the utmost of upward currents athwart topmost boughs. There is a spiralling, thistle-down lightness about the ascents from and return to tree summits pleasant to watch and the slow-floating demonstrations recur many times on a bright courtship morning. The birds are rarely near the ground; they like to perch high with wings half-spread, as though poised more on the wind than supported by the twigs. They collect in small wandering parties to clean the trees of parasitic grubs and on quiet evenings sail with balancing, deliberate flight to capture insects in the air. Lesser woodland residents raise a clamour against the arrival of the cuckoo-shrikes; and the big birds respond with low, thick, slurred notes which sound fretfully disinterested. Common names for the species are 'Blue Jay' and, in Tasmania, 'Summer bird'.

BLACK-FACED CUCKOO-SHRIKE

NATURAL SIZE 13″   *Reproduced about* 1/4 *natural size*

RED WATTLE BIRD *Anthochaera carunculata*

RECOGNITION: Southern Q'ld, N.S.W., Vic., S.A., south-western
Aus. Harsh and husky; boldly streaked white;
red spot below and behind eye. (2)

DESCRIPTION: 14. Brown-grey; on shoulder, below eye and under
parts, lighter; streaked white above and below;
mid-abdomen yellow; tail tipped white; legs
brown-grey; bill black; iris red.

The voice of the wattle bird in the scrub is as harmonious as a
cougher at a concert; it vies with the Friar birds in obstructed
and dissonant notes, rasps and harsh croaks, as if it were a
perpetual sufferer from sore throat. Occasionally an uneasy
whistle breaks through the untuneful symphony. Long-
tailed and inclined to be ragged-looking, the bird peers
sinuously as it climbs in eucalypts, and particularly banksias,
for nectar and insects. It is incongruous that this weighty,
almost cumbersome, fellow has to be classified with the usually
lissom, melodious and dexterous honeyeaters. In flight the
Red Wattle Bird's silhouette is attenuated, the rounded wings
beating in uneven rhythm, then being held in a glide. The
yellow on the belly is a more obvious mark of identification
than the fleshy wattle under the face conferring the name.
The birds wander, and in the winter months are sighted in
more open country. Where garden owners are complacent,
Red Wattle Birds drop into the flower-beds as a snack bar,
scrambling among honeysuckles and swaying giddily on
delphinium stalks as they delve for nectar.

RED WATTLE BIRD

LITTLE WATTLE BIRD *Anthochaera chrysoptera*

RECOGNITION: Southern Q'ld, N.S.W., Vic., S.A., south-western
Aus., Tas. Spotted white on chest; reddish-brown
wing patch when flying; no wattle. (2)

DESCRIPTION: 11. Brown-grey; upper parts streaked; under parts
spotted; chestnut on wing in flight; tail tipped
white; legs blackish; bill dark brown; iris red-
brown.

Lesser size and the absence of yellow tinge on the belly single
out this wattle bird, though the plumage and calls have a
cousinly resemblance to those of the Red Wattle Bird. Being
smaller, the Little Wattle Bird is more neatly active, but both
have the same sinewy, contorted movements—like the
cormorants and a few other species, wattle birds give a hint
of the presumed origin of all birds from a reptilian stock. That
does not prevent the Little Wattle Bird from determinedly
harrying the largest brown or tiger snake. He is very game,
and has a leisurely, teasing humour towards other birds. With
human beings he is fairly discreet; his flight to cover is quick,
low and direct. Once there, raucous, brittle calls retreat and
fade away. Between the ugly cries of the Red and Little
Wattle Birds there is not much to choose. Gould says the
lesser bird reminded the aborigines of a man being sick;
the name they give was 'Goo-gwar-ruck'. 'Keek-kiweek' is
one favourite call and landings on a tree limb may be completed by a chattering exclamation. The voice, then, is
uncouth and the plumage not remarkable; yet in the sober
embroidery of feather there is attractiveness.

LITTLE WATTLE BIRD

NATURAL SIZE 11″   *Reproduced about 1/4 natural size*

NOISY MINER   *Myzantha melanocephala*

RECOGNITION: Q'ld, N.S.W., Vic., S.A. and Tas. Yellow patch behind eye; garrulous, full of commotion. (2)

DESCRIPTION: 10. Grey; wing and tail coverts brownish-grey, greenish on wing secondaries; forehead whitish; crown and about ear black; breast mottled grey, abdomen white; yellow skin triangle behind eye; legs and bill yellow; iris brown.

'Soldier bird' is a popular name for this tree sentinel and gossip. Like an inquisitive peeper behind curtains, he squints anxiously through the leaves to see what goes on in the village and who is coming along the street. 'Soldiers' keep together in small platoons; as the motorist drives along the highways he will catch them fluttering up from the grass verges to a handy look-out bough. With other birds the Noisy Miner officiously stands on his rights; a busybody himself, he is vexed if others pry or interfere, and there are frequent uproars with the neighbours. Talkative enough when peacefully together, in a fight the birds raise lusty battle-cries; amid all the vociferation there may be a few accidentally pleasing sounds. The mixture of old-womanish curiosity and swagger makes the 'Soldier' a comical creature. Noisy Miners are insectivorous, hunting through the trees and on the ground; they also feed on native fruits and berries. The spelling, incidentally, might well be reformed to 'Mynah', since the bird was named with the Indian Mynah in mind. The Soldier Bird has a popular reputation for reporting the progress of snakes, and an unpopular one for the same alertness if gunners are on the prowl.

NOISY MINER

NATURAL SIZE 10″   *Reproduced about 1/3 natural size*

COMMON MYNAH   *Acridotheres tristis*

RECOGNITION: Eastern Aus. Yellow patch behind eye; plumply brown and black; white wing discs. (5)

DESCRIPTION: 10. Head and neck black, rest of body warm brown, paling on belly; outer flight feathers darker brown, with white patches at base shown as circles in flight; rounded tail broadly tipped white, except for two centre feathers; legs, and fleshy wattle below and behind eye, bright yellow; iris reddish-brown.

The Common Mynah, India's most prevalent bird, has been taken to New Zealand, South Africa and other countries because of its fondness for noxious grubs and insects. Despite their native 'burning plains', the birds appear to feel high Australian temperatures and have mostly spread through the cooler south-eastern areas, with a preference for settled places; they are, however, common in parts of north-eastern Queensland, where they were introduced to combat the sugar-cane beetle. The mynah is irrepressible and humorous in voice and behaviour. He will buffoon with a sheet of newspaper found m the gutter or, full of precaution, creep up to pull the tail of a companion; and squatting by his mate, throw her a mixture of gurgling, hectoring notes, with peering looks and epileptic bobbings of the head. The birds keep in pairs, with some autumn and winter flocking. The Common Mynah's marriage is an affectionate association. The partners feed together—worms, caterpillars, fruit, corn, cattle parasites, little comes amiss; they preen each other's feathers, officiously patrol their territory and converse with gusto. Mynahs often join forces with that other brisk opportunist, the Starling.

COMMON MYNAH

NATURAL SIZE 10″   *Reproduced about 1/3 natural size*

EASTERN WHIPBIRD *Psophodes olivaceus*

RECOGNITION: Northern Q'ld to southern Vic. Swish and loud whip-crack from close cover. (2)

DESCRIPTION: 10. Upper parts dull green; head, crest, breast and throat black; white patches side of gullet; abdomen white with dark mottling; tail margined white; legs and bill black; iris red.

It is troublesome to get a close-up of the Eastern Whipbird. In the sense that many have heard it, the bird is common, yet for ten persons who have listened only one may have managed to observe its curious performance. No more than two glimpses in doubtful light rewarded a forty-eight hour camp by the Ovens, where a pair skulked in a thick brake—and in other places whipbirds have been in equally unaccommodating mood. They shift within their mazes of foliage without trace—silent in movement, but ironically loud of voice. The voice cannot be mistaken: the lash and smack of the invisible whip would not be bettered on a stock route. Two long warning whistles culminate in the vehement whizz and crack, and two exclamatory notes, sounding like 'Choo-choo', round off a circus-ring act. The two-note finale is usually uttered by the female, but if she is hesitant the male may complete the performance. When the point from which a whipbird signals has been approached, the next slash will probably be aimed from an entirely new bearing. If, as is said, the birds spend much time turning over litter on the ground, their investigation is noiseless. The Western Whipbird's song is guttural and the explosive crack is absent.

EASTERN WHIPBIRD

NATURAL SIZE 10″   *Reproduced about 1/3 natural size*

BLACKBIRD *Turdus merula*

RECOGNITION: N.S.W., Vic., S.A., Tas. All black; orange bill; profuse, varied, mellow song. (1,2)

DESCRIPTION: 10. Glossy black; bill and eye-rim orange; legs blackish; iris dark brown. *Female*, dark brown, paler throat, breast rufous, streaked darker; legs and bill dark brown.

The famous European singer has founded himself in gardens, parks and scrubs of the cooler regions. The male is jaunty, suspicious, pugnacious and handsome; as he alights, he raises his tail as if in challenge and to show it off. The alarm note is a jumbled, panicky scream, usually given as the bird hurries away; 'tac' is a repeated note as he prepares to roost; and chinking and chuckling calls accompany the activities and excursions of the day. The diet, like that of other thrushes, includes snails, certain slugs, grubs, worms and insects. Wild berries are eagerly raided. In summer, blackbirds' interests extend to the fruit on trees they have helped to keep pest-free throughout the winter. In Tasmania, where the climate has fostered their number, some orchard owners regrettably kill all comers. As a musician the Blackbird is a composer of genius. Birds ordinarily borrow, mimic and reiterate set notes and phrases. The Blackbird improvises on a theme. At the opening of the singing months, from late July or August to January or February, the male softly experiments with the motive. Thereafter his perfected tune, often hauntingly lovely, underlies the season's singing—modulated, varied, now withheld, now seductively reintroduced. The voice is fluting, cool and effortless, crowned by a leisurely, happy serenity. Of all bird song, the Blackbird comes nearest to humanly contrived intervals and melodies; many consider that he writes the supreme score.

BLACKBIRD

NATURAL SIZE 10″   *Reproduced about* 1/3 *natural size*

FAN-TAILED CUCKOO *Cacomantis flabelliformis*

RECOGNITION: Aus., except north-western and central. Far-carrying, shivering call, descending scale; slate mantle, tail notched white, brown breast. (1,2)

DESCRIPTION: 10. Upper parts blue-black, tail feathers tipped and indented with white, especially under. Breast rust-rufous; throat and on belly grey; legs olive-yellow; bill curved, black, lighter at base; iris dark brown. *Young*, varying tones of brown; noticeable white hatching on tail.

In many neighbourhoods the continual, rather mournful cadence of the Fan-tail ('That strain again! it had a dying fall') is the proclamation of spring. The purring, vibrating trill from the bough is produced with energy, with wide-open beak and half-open, trembling wings, often in plain view in orchard trees which have not yet put on their leaves. On moonlight and mild nights the sound rings through the dark hours; and as the season matures, the cuckoo adds a smooth, dreary whistle. Overcast and threatening skies prompt the bird to protest against, or perhaps approve, the gloom. Its temperament seems rather melancholy; only when a pair have newly succeeded in 'planting' an egg do they appear in good heart. If approached, the birds linger, as though injured at having to move. In every way, the Fan-tail is the reverse of radiant; its fastidious dress is quietly beautiful. The lightly wooded country in which the birds are obvious is deserted in winter, probably for denser cover and warmer parts of the cuckoo range. Insects are hunted and caterpillars picked off bark, leaves and weeds. The depositing of eggs in foster-parents' nests may be by laying them direct, inserting them by the bill or, according to a Tasmanian report, by dropping the egg from the claws. A very broad range of species is victimized.

FAN-TAILED CUCKOO

NATURAL SIZE 10″   *Reproduced about 1/3 natural size*

PALLID CUCKOO   *Cuculus pallidus*

RECOGNITION: Aus. Semitone bird; half a dozen to a dozen monosyllabic calls running up the scale. (2)

DESCRIPTION: 12. Upper parts brownish-grey, shoulder-patch
white, wing spotted white, outer tail feathers
notched white; under parts pale grey, underwing
browner, barred white; legs blackish-grey; bill
blackish-brown; iris brown. *Female*, colouring less
smoothly uniform, mottled and spotted chestnut.

Like most cuckoos the Pallid Cuckoo has a highly distinctive
voice to broadcast news of spring. The series of short, separate,
rising notes, like a wood-wind player inaccurately flitting up
the scale, is repeated by day and night and has earned this
bird the name belonging to the Hawk-Cuckoo of India and
Ceylon—Brain Fever bird. That somewhat similar, same-
sized cuckoo with an ascending repetition really does,
however, seem to shout 'Brain fever!' As monotonous as the
Pallid male's piping is the female's blaring, husky 'Kheer'.
She also, when manoeuvring to board out her eggs, uses a
trill and excited, explosive cries. The Pallid Cuckoo is more
arboreal and less easily watched than the Fan-tail, his co-
announcer of spring. The looping flight as the birds inspect
other species' nests is quickly recognized; wings and body
show ashen against the bright spring skies. Honeyeaters are
most victimized, but the cuckoos have a wide list of slave
foster-parents for voracious youngsters whose imperious
'Zwit' calls harass the bush in early summer. The Semitone
bird is a useful insect destroyer, having the true cuckoo
appetite for hairy caterpillars which other finders shun. In
migration from the north the males precede their mates.

PALLID CUCKOO

INDIAN TURTLE-DOVE   *Streptopelia chinensis*

RECOGNITION: Aus. Warm brown and grey; black patches, conspicuously spotted white, sides and back of neck. (1,5)

DESCRIPTION: 12. Back and wings brown, mottled rufous, outer edge of wing greyer, quills brown; middle tail feathers brown, the rest black with white tips; top and sides of head vinous grey; throat whitish; hind neck and sides black, each feather ending in two white spots; under parts vinous; undertail whitish; legs pinky-red; bill lead colour; iris hazel.

Introduced towards the end of last century, the Spotted Dove, which ranges eastward from India to China, has colonized several Australian areas. It drinks copiously, likes to be near water, and mainly bases itself on the cities and towns. One pays a little in young shoots and seedlings for its decorative company near the house. The mild, hoarse 'Ku-kroo-ku' is a soothing sound in parks and gardens. The turtle-dove is an attractive bird either in flight or on the ground, where the search for seeds largely keeps it. The pairs are constant and probably mate for life. If disturbed on the lawn they spring straight up with a whirr and commotion for five or six feet, then level off in swift flight, the wings flicking stiffly, and the partly spread tail displaying its white fringe. The journey soon slants down to a landing on a branch or on the grass. Abrupt upward flights and return glides, with the tail rigidly fanned, are noticeable in the courtship months and husband and wife continue demonstrably affectionate the year round. Quick to gobble household scraps, they are gluttons also for sun and rain, angling their wings and half-dislocating their backs to trap warmth or moisture inside their plumage.

INDIAN TURTLE-DOVE

WEDGE-TAILED EAGLE *Uroaëtus audax*

RECOGNITION: Aus. Soaring, kingly; wing span about seven feet; long wedge-tail obvious. (1,2)

DESCRIPTION: 36. Blackish; nape light or dark brown marked black, rump sometimes whitish; legs feathered, toes light grey; beak brownish-grey; iris hazel. *Immature* birds, more streaked and margined buff, brown and chestnut. *Female*, 40

As an Englishman must travel to Australia to admire something akin to his once familiar White-tailed Eagle, so tomorrow's Australian may visit other continents to see the grandeur his forefathers destroyed. Like a dog with a bad name, the Wedge-tailed Eagle is apparently saddled permanently with the reputation of lamb-killer. The food of this formidable bird consists mostly of rabbits, carrion, lizards and, as with the Tawny Eagle of India, prey bullied from hawks and hunting animals. Some State Governments continue to offer blood-money and many landholders still think no method too barbarous to exterminate their country's most majestic bird. Despite exact evidence that the eagle does more good than harm, eager exaggerations of damage, and unmerciful slaughter, continue. On the ground the lolloping run or walk is awkward. Travelling through the air, banking and soaring without a beat, or changing course with a few impulses of the great wings to begin a vast glide, the Wedgetail is gloriously master. In lonely back areas the bird will remain perched, stern and dignified, until at fifty yards the observer can view the flattened head, curved beak and brooding eye. People must go farther and farther afield to study one of the birds of the world that fires well ordered imaginations. Australia's eagle, an aristocrat, must be kept from the fate of the Lammergeier in the Alps or of the Osprey and Sea Eagle in Britain.

WEDGE–TAILED EAGLE

NATURAL SIZE 36″

Reproduced about 1/7 natural size

125

WHISTLING EAGLE *Haliastur sphenurus*

RECOGNITION: Aus. Staccato, crescendo whistling, airy and shrill; usually near salt or fresh water. (3,4)

DESCRIPTION: 21. Back and wings dark brown, spotted pale buff; quills blackish; head lighter; tail greyish-brown; under parts tawny brown, buff streaked; legs yellowish-white; beak brown; iris light brown.

The aerial whistle, 'Chew-few-few', a rushing, rising, windy note, often announces the identity of this buoyant hawk; it must be one of the noisiest raptorial birds. Another pointer is its fondness for water. Along channels and drains it quarters the reed beds like a harrier, snatching rats, lizards and smaller prey. Sunlight displays its handsome sandy, chestnut and almost black tints, the lighter tone of the head and tail being noticeable. At some ports, such as Townsville, the hawks swing over the roof tops in companies of four or five, and cruise alertly about the harbour for scraps. Floating debris is clawed up and, if useless, dropped; a savoury catch the bird will eat on the wing, bending its head to its talons. Awkwardly large prizes may be flown to a perch and dissected. On the plains of New South Wales, far from the nearest water of the Darling, I have seen the birds systematically hunting, presumably for rabbits, which they help to keep down. In similarly dry country they will feed on the remains of cattle and sheep. The Whistling Eagle sometimes is stupidly destroyed for no better reason than that it possesses a hooked beak. The female bird is an inch or more larger than the male. These eagles are now being moved into the category of kites, to whose attentive scavenging habits along the beaches and inland they certainly conform.

WHISTLING EAGLE

NATURAL SIZE 21"   *Reproduced about 1/5 natural size*

SWAMP HARRIER *Circus approximans*

RECOGNITION: Aus. Medley of browns; white band across tail; beats low and heavily over water. (4)

DESCRIPTION: 20. Darkish brown above, more buff about neck and shoulders, grey-brown on black-barred tail; under parts buff, streaked and barred darker brown or grey-brown; legs yellow-green; bill black; iris brown.

The tones and markings of the brown plumage vary considerably, but the Swamp Harrier is a self-identifying bird as it sails a foot or two above the rushes of a lake or combs the rows of a tall crop. Swimming fowl are sometimes snatched; coots and dabchicks dive as the harrier swerves over; and snakes and vermin are pounced on at the verges of the water. At Purrumbeete Lake, Victoria, a half-live rat, dropped from a harrier's talons, nearly struck my up-turned face. This patroller of marsh and cover has none of the dash of the aerial hunter: it is a dogged searcher; a bold, imposing and useful hawk.

SPOTTED HARRIER *Circus assimilis*

RECOGNITION: Aus. Darker, smokier, plumage more 'curdled' looking; rufous and spotted under. (1)

DESCRIPTION: 21. Upper parts grey-brown, wing coverts mottled brown, quills black; tail grey, barred darker, tipped lighter; crown and facial disc rufous; under parts reddish-brown, much spotted white; legs yellow; bill black; iris yellow.

In dry areas this is the more likely hawk, but Spotted may join Swamp Harriers around water to make a maze of fifty big birds playing in the air. The two harriers will hunt and perch together. Low, deliberate inspection round scrub and trees is varied by soaring excursions. Rabbits, mice, lizards and large insects are captured; the harrier may be surprised at his meal on the ground. The female hawk is the larger.

SWAMP HARRIER

SPOTTED HARRIER

NATURAL SIZE 20″-21″   *Reproduced about 1/8 natural size*

BLACK-SHOULDERED KITE   *Elanus axillaris*

RECOGNITION: Aus. Hovers like Kestrel. Light, delicate grey, with broad black patch on upper wing. (1)

DESCRIPTION: 14. Above, gull grey, shading darker on wing primaries; shoulder area, obvious black patch; slight black in front of eye; under parts white, except for dark blur, as though shoulder markings were showing through; small black underwing marking at base of outer quills; legs and cere yellow; bill black; iris deep orange.

The only hawk for which this bird is likely to be mistaken is the Letter-winged Kite which is less common and has black markings forming a prominent underwing pattern. The neatness with which the Black-shouldered Kite hovers—the Kestrel's nearest challenger in that accomplishment—is a sure identification. This bird, of ghostly colouring, with dark epaulettes, is more sturdily built than the·Kestrel and shows a little less grace and finish, both when 'waiting on' and in the glides with which the falcon passes to a fresh observation point. Alone or in pairs, the birds are usually seen hunting in open or lightly wooded country; but I have watched a kite cross the gardens of a Melbourne suburb and they are not shy of farms and country townships. The kite shares the Kestrel's diet as well as its habits. Large numbers of mice are taken. This is another beautiful bird of prey which only the fool with a gun will shoot. It moves south in winter. Numbers vary noticeably from year to year and in unpredictable seasons the hunters have been abundant enough in the southeast to set the uninformed asking questions. Increasing reports of winter birds on the outskirts of Melbourne suggest resident inclinations.

BLACK-SHOULDERED KITE

FORK-TAILED KITE   *Milvus migrans*

RECOGNITION: Aus. Large, dark gliding hawk, with tail forked. (1)

DESCRIPTION: 22. Upper parts brown-black, plumage margined lighter; wing quills black; some whitish head feathers; tail brown, barred black; under parts rufous, streaked black; legs yellow; beak slatey black; iris brown.

When prospecting for snakes, small animals or for a dead wombat or wallaby killed by a truck on the road, the Fork-tailed or Black Kite sweeps, circles and glides low, then moves on with deliberate beat. But when it soars, rejoicing in a thunder-storm or blustering wind, it has the ease and lift, and more than the lightness, of an eagle. It is north of the Tropic of Capricorn that the bird starts to be common. Five or six may sit on a tree, as composed as starlings. Near Darwin I have watched three hundred or more in the air—a blizzard of kites, in which it was hard to single out the course of any one. Aloft, they look dark, the rich reddish under-markings showing only in favourable lights. The Fork-tailed or Black Kite has come to Britain at least twice from Africa or Europe and is closely akin to the Red Kite, which Shakespeare's Autolycus mentions, and which from ancient times until the middle of last century was a confident scavenger in city and village. Thanks to the gamekeeper, then to the 'oologist', avid for the last British clutches, the birds were reduced to half a dozen in mid-Wales. Yearly watch against the vandal has given numbers some chance to rebuild and pairs have tried to extend the range into England. In Australia the Black Kite, which disposes of carrion and offal, is no less interesting, harmless and helpful. The call is a weak mewing cry. Young birds are less dark and are boldly streaked with buff.

FORK-TAILED KITE

NATURAL SIZE 22"   *Reproduced about 1/5 natural size*

KESTREL *Falco cenchroides*

RECOGNITION: Aus. Poises in mid-air, wings winnowing, then
               extended motionless; head bent, tail fanned—
               Windhover. (1)

DESCRIPTION: 12. Above light warm brown to rose-colour,
               feathers centred black; wing quills darker; tail
               ashy, broad black sub-terminal band tipped white;
               under parts whitish, breast streaked variable brown;
               skin round eye and cere yellow; legs orange-
               yellow; bill blue-grey; iris brown.

Better than any other bird the Windhover has mastered the
trick of suspending itself in the wind's eye, alternately
silhouetting its wings in an almost unmoving arc, then flailing
the air to regain height or luffing up to maintain station.
Having raked a patch with sight that distinguishes more at
fifty feet than human vision at as many inches, the little falcon
either plummets down, the long pinions almost closed, to
grasp its mouthful, or slants, often without a beat, to the next
paddock. Frequently the marking process is disrupted by
mobbing crows, magpies or smaller fry; then the Kestrel
tilts aside or lifts with an absent-minded, contemptuous
deftness. If the attack grows wearisome, it may loose a high,
angry chatter, and, half rolling over, strike at its assailant
with its talons. The Kestrel hunts wherever there are rodents,
lizards, grasshoppers, beetles and other insects—with a small
snake, leveret or bird as change of food. Only unknowing,
rank stupidity wars—because of its classification among the
birds of prey—with a hawk at once so graceful and so useful.
The persistent mistake of calling this most beneficial bird a
'sparrow hawk'—it differs entirely—encourages blockheads
to destroy.

KESTREL

NATURAL SIZE 12″   *Reproduced about 1/4 natural size*

BROWN HAWK *Falco berigora*

RECOGNITION: Aus. All shades of variegated brown; often perches on trees and overhead wires. (1,2)

DESCRIPTION: 17. Upper parts dark brown, spotted rufous, tail barred rufous; breast dark brown; throat, belly, underwing and undertail buffish-brown; black moustache-stripe base of beak to below eye; naked skin about eye, pale blue; legs and beak blue-grey; iris brown. *Female*, about an inch longer.

Most of the raptorial birds have variable plumage and few are less uniform than this often-seen hawk, which in its dark aspect may be chocolate-black, in its lighter forms show pallid buff or white under-feathers, or which may be mottled rust or cinnamon. Though enumerated with falcons, it has little of their haughty bearing when perched, and the flight is too indecisive and deliberate to compare with falcon surety and power. Like the Kestrel, the Brown Hawk lives on snakes, mice, the occasional small bird, grasshoppers, beetles and other insects; these are captured by pouncing rather than by pursuit. While it might be an over-statement that no newly-hatched farm chick has ever been taken to feed hungry young, it is right to certify these hawks as mainly harmless and useful. To shoot birds that happen to circle near a house is sentence before evidence. The Brown Hawk's planing and soaring over tree-tops and wide paddocks is one of the sights of the countryside; and elderly country people say it is less common than a generation ago. It has a grating, cackling call and is sometimes known as the 'Cackling Hawk'. At nesting time it may take over serviceable old habitations of the crow and magpie.

BROWN HAWK

NATURAL SIZE 17"   *Reproduced about 1/4 natural size*

137

BOOBOOK   *Ninox boobook*

RECOGNITION: Aus. except Tas. Calls name, sometimes translated
as 'Mopoke' or 'More Pork'. (2)

DESCRIPTION: 15. Upper parts dark brown, mottled white on
wings; under parts cinnamon and buff, streaked
white; chin white; legs feathered, feet light grey;
bill slate; iris yellowish or grey-green.

If traced to its day-time perch in the bush, this owl, with erect
'whiskers', cat-like glare and brows compressed into a
menacing frown, looks balefully hostile and blunders off into
deeper recesses. After dark it does not always resent observation. One bird came boldly out of riverside timber to the
parapet of a bridge to stand sentry for night-flying insects,
ghosting after them into the full illumination of the street
lamps. The tenor calls are a distant parody of the European
cuckoo's notes, yet lack their fluting, human quality.

BARN OWL   *Tyto Alba*

RECOGNITION: Aus. Will hunt by day in breeding season; white
face and under parts show in dusk; snoring, rasping
screech. (1,2)

DESCRIPTION: 14. Upper parts grey-brown, mottled white and
black; under parts white, finely dotted dark brown;
facial disc white; legs feathered, feet brown-grey;
bill whitish; iris dark brown.

This beautifully clad owl will hover near in the last light to
stare with an uncanny, Mephistophelian look into your face.
The brown head feathers end like a line of human hair across
the forehead and the dark division of the face above the bill
heightens the suggestion of a nose. Despite its eerie scrutinies
of an observer and chilling screech, the hunter is harmless—
no worse than a floating terrier for rats, mice, house-sparrows,
beetles and other insects. In England barns were left with
special nesting apertures. Here distribution is very local.

BOOBOOK

BARN OWL

NATURAL SIZE 14″-15″   *Reproduced about 1/7 natural size*

139

TAWNY FROGMOUTH *Podargus strigoides*

RECOGNITION: Aus. Mottled, wooden, freezes as tree fragment when resting by day. (2)

DESCRIPTION: 16. Upper parts grey, with varied smoky browns, spotted white on wings; under parts ashy brown, lined and blotched blackish-brown; legs grey-brown; bill grey; gape provided with bristles; iris yellow-brown.

Handsomely-variegated neutral plumage wonderfully conceals this outlandish-looking night bird in its brooding through the sunny hours. It becomes a very part of its roost, the stretched, attenuated attitude of its body simulating the outline of a snapped branch or stump, as the feathers mimic the indeterminate shading of the wood. To blunder on a dozing Frogmouth in the bush startles observer and bird. There is a feeling of disquiet in being watched in return by the almost closed slits of yellow eyes. At dusk the bird tenses to its vigil, the lean body assuming a squat, toad-like silhouette on the bough from which it pores over the ground for the slightest significant stir. A noiseless drop, deliberate yet speedy, and a mouse or small organism that moved is in the gaping mouth. The Frogmouth is said, as an unusual exercise, to call like a Boobook owl. But its normal note, or grunt, is a stertorous, pumping 'Oom, oom, oom,' wound up to ten, twenty, or forty iterations. The sketchy nest may be isolated on a bare limb, the female brooding lengthwise along the branch and appearing only an excrescence on bark and wood. If confronted, this 'owl' that is not an owl struggles to look more sinister than a Tasmanian devil—feathers stiffened, eyes dilated and bill gaped to present the startling yellow throat. But one finishes an inspection without damage.

TAWNY FROGMOUTH

NATURAL SIZE 16″   *Reproduced about 1/4 natural size*

KOOKABURRA *Dacelo gigas*

RECOGNITION: Q'ld, N.S.W., Vic., S.A., introduced W.A., Tas. Cackling, noisy laughter; hulking, squat; heavy bill. (1,2)

DESCRIPTION: 17. Upper parts mottled brown, lighter at head and rump; pale blue on shoulder and wing; tail barred black, white terminal band in flight; crown dark marks, slight crest; from bill through eye dark streak; under parts and nape whitish; legs pale brown; bill blackish above, whitish below; iris pale brown.

Everything about the Laughing Jackass hints at powerfulness —the raucous, uproarious gusts of laughter; the strong, dangerous-looking bill; the bulky, muscular frame. Like certain gulls, the bird has forsaken a fisherman's life to become a landlubber; it preys on small mammals, insects and their larvae, the young of other birds and, occasionally, snakes. The Kookaburra is a national emblem and, aware of the favourable sentiment, will become a pensioner on the door-step. But he will be expensive to other garden birds; these fear and some-times mob the big oppressor. The jackass flies with rapid directness, often hugging the ground. He is not particularly active and will pass a long half-hour rooted to a branch, indifferent to uneasy surrounding chatter. Only his head appears alive, as the neck is twisted, owl-fashion, almost through a complete circle. Abruptly he may drop to the ground, bolt a morsel and swing to another vantage. The bouts of mirth, in which some people fancy they detect malice and others only roystering good humour, may infect several jackasses. The spasms come on at any time, but mostly at sunrise and sunset. They have a whirring prelude, or wind-up, to the top pitch of half-guttural, half-screaming notes; and when these have slowed and almost died away, the fit may revive and the racket flare up anew.

KOOKABURRA

WHITE COCKATOO   *Kakatoë galerita*

RECOGNITION: Aus. except west, south of Fitzroy River, and Tas. White, yellow crest; large, loudly screeching. (2)

DESCRIPTION: 20. White, except for prominent crest; underwing and undertail, sulphur; legs and beak light to dark grey; iris black.

The parrot order is credited with more brain than other races of birds. White Cockatoos show their intelligence by posting scouts when the main body has settled to feed, especially if on forbidden crops; the sentinels make near approach impossible. Like crows, they appear to gauge whether a human being carries a weapon. Any considerable gathering is quickly noticeable. Perched amid sombre foliage they stand out like toys on a Christmas tree; and, when the torpedo-bodies and rounded wings are in the air, the upper plumage flashes like snow in the sun while the under-feathers, with their wash of sulphur colour, look dense and opaque. The birds perch together in silence, watching with black, attentive eye and raising and lowering their crests; or, swarming in the air, maintain a dizzy screeching and screaming. The grinding voice charms no-one, but the united choir of these strident throats is like the crash and grating draw of waves on shingle. Eye and ear are baffled by the swirling noise and whirling wings till the senses are half gratified by the sheer tumult. White Cockatoos keep in the neighbourhood of timber; they eat roots and seeds and sometimes raid crop sowings. A prolonged visit by these formidable samplers will leave a keen gardener short-tempered.

WHITE COCKATOO

NATURAL SIZE 20″   *Reproduced about 1/6 natural size*

GANG-GANG COCKATOO   *Callocephalon fimbriatus*

RECOGNITION: N.S.W., Vic., Tas. Dusky; face and 'ruffed up'
crown brick-red; 'grating hinge' cry. *Female*, no
red on head. (2)

DESCRIPTION: $13\frac{1}{2}$. Barrings of deep smoky grey and lighter grey,
browner on breast and belly, greenish tinges on
wing; head and crest red to pink; legs and bill
medium grey; iris black.

The noisy Gang-Gang is heard afar as it clambers the trees
for gum-seeds or flaps across the valley—a wheezing, rusty
voice harsh as a hinge on a swinging door. Human beings
it may treat disdainfully. Cones were cast from a *radiata* pine
beneath which I was watching with an accuracy (the cockatoos
meanwhile peering down) hard to accept as purely coinci-
dental. The rosy countenance, topped by an uncombed,
careless crest gives the Gang-Gang a high-foreheaded,
weirdly intellectual look, which is enhanced by the penetrating
white-rimmed eyes. Etched and cross-lined, the plumage is
like eddying smoke. Hawthorn thickets are a banquet for the
Gang-Gangs when the hips and haws have turned colour. The
birds swarm over the bushes, plucking bunches of berries,
gluttonously cracking the stones and growling dog-like as
they munch. Berries not of exact ripeness are spat out;
sometimes the stones are swallowed, sometimes discarded.
Pairs keep close together while sharing the meal and a
moderate flock will turn half an acre of autumn-loaded thorns
into 'bare ruined choirs' in an hour's visit. Dense and lightly
timbered regions are the home of these cockatoos.

146

GANG-GANG COCKATOO

GALAH   *Kakatoë roseicapilla*

RECOGNITION: Aus., rarely in Tas. Rose and grey; dense flocks inland. (1)

DESCRIPTION: 14. Back, wings and tail, light grey, darker on wing quills and tip of tail; neck and head pinky-white, slight crest; under body and edge of underwing rich pink; rest of underwing and undertail grey; legs grey; beak whitish; iris brown.

In flat open country an immense flock of these cockatoos may rise from a paddock, alternately showing the pink of their under-plumage, then the delicate greys of the upper feathers. They make a rosy cloud, a resplendent sight when the colouring is thrown up against ranks of trees. As the multitude swirls away, there will be a huge clamour—the calls that gave rise to the nickname 'Willie-willock'. The colonies keep mostly to the interior; but isolated birds may pass over townships and coastal country. Seeds and roots are the Galah's staple food and as a weed controller he does incalculable good. The extension of his diet to include grain has put him on the black list in the wheat belts and many thousands are wiped out year by year to earn vermin money. In the field a feeding flock is protected by a sentry and wavers off at the alarm tumultuously crying, with changes of direction (no-one knows on what drill order or impulse) as one. In a north Victorian town thousands of these beautifully tinted birds were collected annually to stage a revolting corroboree for trap shooters. Slowly gathering sentiment towards wild life has goaded the State Government into stopping the 'sport' at last.

GALAH

NATURAL SIZE 14″   *Reproduced about 1/4 natural size*

RED-TAILED BLACK COCKATOO *Calyptorhynchus banksii*

RECOGNITION: Aus. Shining black; in flight panels of red on tail. (2)

DESCRIPTION: 24. Black, with glowing red sub-terminal tail band except on central feathers; legs grey-black; bill black; iris brown. *Female* and *immature males*, spotted and barred yellow, tail barred orange.

Flying in sunlight, these large cockatoos look exotic and glorious; the plumage scintillates, but loses nothing of its dense jet black, and the red oblongs in the tail glow like the pane of a cathedral window. Mostly the Red-tailed Black Cockatoo is glimpsed amid the trees in pairs or small flocks, but in lonely country I have surprised hundreds of the birds. Wave after wave, they rose in scores and fifties on hurried, rounded wings, streaming across the scrubby plain with a clamour that made the air alive, as with the vibration of clashing bells. In full massed chorus, the sounds have a wild melody; but the solitary call—a grating 'Krurr'—is not pleasing. The bird feeds on native seeds and grubs; it causes no anxiety to fruit growers. It may be mistaken for the Glossy Black Cockatoo which has similar tail markings and ranges down the eastern side of the continent into South Australia, but the Glossy Black is a smaller bird, less intensely black. The Yellow-tailed and White-tailed Black Cockatoos—the last confined to south-western Australia—are browner and, in comparison with the Red-tailed Black, appear dingy. These birds pay for their footing in the forests. Although they wrench bark and scarify trunks, they relieve the trees of an enormous and assorted infestation.

RED–TAILED BLACK
COCKATOO

CRIMSON ROSELLA   *Platycercus elegans*

RECOGNITION: Q'ld, N.S.W., Vic. Prevailing hue crimson. (2)

DESCRIPTION: 14. Under parts, head, neck and rump, glowing
red; back dusky blue-black flecked red; tail, throat,
shoulders and wing primaries lighter blue, quills
blackish-brown; legs black; bill bluish-white;
iris black. *Young*, green on back, variable.

The simple contrast of two gorgeous colours, deep red and
lush blue, makes this in some eyes a more strikingly beautiful
bird than several of the more diversely marked parrots.
Hesitant when aware of being watched, Red Lories nevertheless pay visits to capital cities; in Melbourne I have seen birds
alight in unfrequented streets and in Sydney have looked up
to find them flying as pace-makers to a suburban train. The
rosellas often come to the ground to eat seeds and, possibly,
grubs; when half-hidden in fruit and berry bushes a rich
chuckling and full clear notes may give away their presence.
On my drive-way kernels from the fruit of overhanging plum
trees are run over in the summer and compacted into the
surface. During winter Crimson Rosellas patiently ease out
the small nuts, carry them to the bill, almost always with the
left 'hand', crack them audibly and enjoy the contents. But
the birds are found in dense country as well as in open orchard
land. When pairs and small assemblies wander in autumn
they do not come back regularly to the same woodland or
paddocks. They may be absent for three or four years. The
young parrots, patchily green and blue, look comparatively
sombre and rather untidy, as if in the midst of the moult.

CRIMSON ROSELLA

NATURAL SIZE 14″   Reproduced about 1/4 natural size

KING PARROT *Aprosmictus scapularis*

RECOGNITION: Q'ld, N.S.W., Vic. Scarlet and green. (2)

DESCRIPTION: 16. Upper parts rich green; head, neck and under parts scarlet; lower back, rump and tail dark blue; legs blackish; bill pink to red; iris yellow or grey-green. *Female* and *young*, head, upper parts and chest green; bill grey; iris brown.

One of the most superbly clad of the parrots, the King, like the Crimson Rosella, makes an instant impression by its bold dual colouring; in the short-lived flight—often all that one sees of parrots—it is one of the easiest to recognize. But it is interesting if the bird is motionless to perceive how the strong salient colours disperse into admirable camouflage. Leaves and grasses, conflicting light and shade, serve as Nature's blotting paper to mop up the plumage. Though more a bird of the bush and timber than the Crimson Rosella, these parrots pass much time in the same way, searching ground vegetation for seeds. The flight is less agile and dashing than that of most parrots; the King strikes one as a somewhat phlegmatic bird. As well as the usual harsh and boisterous chatter, softer, more musical notes are mingled in flock conversations. The call note is shrill. Growers take toll of this bright raider when it gives trouble in cultivated areas and its numbers may be decreasing.

KING PARROT

NATURAL SIZE 16"   *Reproduced about 1/4 natural size*

EASTERN ROSELLA *Platycercus eximius*

RECOGNITION: Southern Q'ld, Vic., S.A., Tas. White face, red hood, yellow belly. (2)

DESCRIPTION: 12. Crown, nape, neck, breast and vent, bright red; chin and face white; belly yellow; lower abdomen and rump green; back green streaked black; shoulder light blue; tail light blue tipped white; legs grey; bill grey, tip lighter; iris dark brown. *Female*, smaller red hood, more slender.

This gaudy parrot is common, although unevenly distributed. Small flocks swish through the trees with a shrill, beating whistling; when perched they let fall monosyllabic, gentle notes like strokes on a muted bell. Searchers for seeds, berries and fruits, the birds will come down on grass close to a homestead, when the bright raiment can be well scrutinized. The green back, flecked with yellow and with black feather-edges, has a markedly streaked, almost ruffled aspect. If disturbed, they may fly no farther than neighbouring trees or bushes. Moderately wooded country, interspersed with paddocks, suits them well. They may nest, slyly unobtrusive, in a hollow fence-post well within sight of a house, and if the owner has established himself as a tame animal, will reflectively munch his apples almost under his nose. Gould commented aptly on parrots when he declared that no group of birds lent Australia 'so foreign and tropical an air' and he seems to have had this rosella, with its Jacob's coat of many colours, foremost in mind.

EASTERN ROSELLA

NATURAL SIZE 12″   *Reproduced about 1/3 natural size*

157

SWIFT PARROT *Lathamus discolor*

RECOGNITION: Q'ld, N.S.W., Vic., S.A., Tas. Green, picked out
with red on shoulder and about head. (2)

DESCRIPTION: 9½. Upper parts green, blue along wing-edge;
forehead and shoulder red; upper tail coverts blue,
central feathers reddish; under parts yellowish-
green; throat, underwing and under tail coverts
red; legs grey; bill reddish; iris brown.

An elusive parrot, both because of its fast, impetuous streaking
through high foliage and its shifts of country. Eucalypt
flowers provide nectar and food; and the Swifts—whose flocks
often join forces with other species—attend on the readiness
of the trees. But after greedily searching the same bush areas
regularly at blossom-time, the visits may cease for years. The
Swift is one of the more raucous parrots, traceable a long way
by its screaming commotion through the tree-tops; some of
the whistles and warblings used when alighting are diminished
to softer calls. When creeping among the gums for insects and
seeds, and for the nectar of which they are so fond, these active
birds often remain secretively quiet. The long wings and
hurtling passage help to identify this dashing nomad ever on
the track of the honey-flow.

SWIFT PARROT

NATURAL SIZE $9\frac{1}{2}''$ *Reproduced about 1/3 natural size*

RING-NECK PARROT *Barnardius barnardi*

RECOGNITION: Southern Q'ld, N.S.W., north-western Vic., S.A. Yellow collar; vivid green. (2)

DESCRIPTION: 13. Back dark blue; mid-wing green, quills blackish-blue; back of neck collared yellow; forehead banded red; tail green, outer feathers blue, edged white; mid-abdomen orange; chest, belly and undertail pale green; legs black; bill bluish-horn; iris dark brown.

The energetic, numerous Ring-Neck, a clear and brilliant bird of the inland, has yellow-collared relatives, the Port Lincoln and Twenty-Eight Parrots, to carry the range on westwards. In the trees the birds chatter strenuously, gesticulating with their tails and shifting their footholds in animated, argumentative assemblies. 'Tweet-weet' is the call note. There is some foraging in wheat-lands and orchards to vary the seeds and berries diet.

RED-BACKED PARROT *Psephotus haematonotus*

RECOGNITION: Southern Q'ld, N.S.W., Vic., S.A. Upper parts red and green; under parts yellow and green. (1)

DESCRIPTION: 11. Head, throat, tail and mantle green, lower back and rump red; yellow on mid-wing and belly; outer tail feathers white; legs dark grey; bill bluish-grey; iris brown. *Female*, more sober green, no red on back.

In grass country with sparse trees these engaging, merry parrots are often seen in active little parties prowling for seeds along road verges, with the males—the 'red-rumpers'—intermittently bright among the flock. They dash away in brisk and dodging flight, with whistles, half-rasping alarm notes and much chatter, but may soon rest on the highway fencing. They spend many idle hours on paddock wires, sidling up together and chasing each other from the post-tops.

RING-NECK PARROT

RED-BACKED PARROT

NATURAL SIZE 11″-13″   *Reproduced about 1/4 natural size*

WHITE-FACED HERON   *Notophoyx novae-hollandiae*

RECOGNITION: Aus. Grey; lean, long-legged; near water. Flight slow-flapping, methodical, head tucked between shoulders, legs stiffly horizontal. (3)

DESCRIPTION: 25. Upper parts slate-grey, long plumey feathers, mantle in some lights looks blue; forehead, cheek and chin white; upper chest russet; underwing whitish; legs and bare skin round eye greenish-yellow; dagger beak black; iris yellow.

The White-faced Heron or Blue Crane is the common heron of most districts. Whether by a creek bank, on pastures with standing water or perched in thin silhouette on a bough, usually he sees you first and with a loud rasp of annoyance moves off in stately flight. The wing-beats, though they look slow and majestic, are at the rate of about one a second. Although often alone, White-faced Herons are sociable; they nest together in the flat forks of neighbouring trees and sometimes work a river, foreshore or lake margin in company. The birds wade like sleuths till a find can be settled with one pick-axe blow; occasionally several stabs of the bill are needed and a substantial fish may be hauled to higher ground. Rats, mice, small reptiles, frogs, molluscs, insects—especially grass-hoppers and beetles—are hunted, as well as fish. The call note, usually heard when the heron is flying, resembles the 'tear-sheet' sound of the alarm. Aloof and suspicious as herons are, these lonely meditative watchers, who are as much part of their surroundings as the breeze and the water, give life to the rivers and make the swamps less desolate. But breeding colonies are not invariably close to water. Hampered by their sweeping wings and long bills, the parents run an ungainly shuttle service through plantations and among tree branches which have nests islanded among them.

WHITE-FACED HERON

NATURAL SIZE 25″   *Reproduced about 1/8 natural size*

WHITE-NECKED HERON   *Notophoyx pacifica*

RECOGNITION: Aus. Not so common as Blue Crane; more bulky in outline, darker mantle. Habits similar. (3)

DESCRIPTION: 30. Neck, head and breast white, which continues round wing coverts. Remainder blackish-grey, except for slight chestnut on back and upper breast and white streaks on belly; legs and bill black; iris green.

If showing less colour than the Blue Crane, the White-necked Heron is more imposing, not so attenuated in outline. Though I have seen it stalk unconcernedly across the main road of a fair-sized township, it is normally wary, disliking prolonged attention. At an alarm, the neck shoots up or is held rigid—like a periscope—and will be seen to have at the front clearly alternating light and dark markings. This heron is, if possible, a more deliberate, intent hunter than its blue relative. It moves with the caution of a thief on creaking boards, often stopping to watch and, its attitude suggests, to listen fixedly. As a dog thrusts back at the ground with his hind-feet, the big heron periodically rakes the water and the soil at its margin to start small entities from concealment. The stroke of the bill when it comes is as swift as the edging-up process is gradual. The birds' nests, on platforms of sticks in tall trees, may be noticed near water, and sometimes form a small colony. At the sides of the breast herons carry a 'powder puff'—brittle, crumbling feathers of waxy texture—the powder being smoothed on the plumage by the bill, probably as a waterproofing process.

WHITE-NECKED HERON

BROWN BITTERN *Botaurus poiciloptilus*

RECOGNITION: N.S.W., Vic., S.A., W.A. Brown and buff hermit
of the reeds; booms. (3)

DESCRIPTION: 28. Upper parts mottled chocolate, brown and
fawn-gold, greyish on nape and crown; under
parts creamy, streaked dark brown; legs green or
green-yellow; bill brown-yellow; iris hazel.

More people have heard than seen the Bittern. It hides in the
reeds by day, but its resonant deep boom, by night as well as
in daylight hours, carries across two miles. The extraordinary
calls are given in sequence of three or four, male sometimes
responding to male, and they are weighted by a couple of
seconds' pause between each hail, or bellow. Bitterns are
hard to surprise in their watery cover. A bird suddenly
encountered may freeze with stiffly up-pointed neck and bill,
becoming just another reed clump. It may remain with back
turned, motionless, watching over its shoulder; dissolve into
vegetation; or jump and, flying just clear of the wilderness
of stems, drop some distance off. It is hopeless work to trace it
again. The bird's flight is obvious only at breeding time, on
passages for food. The green legs are sloppily dangled at
first; then streamlined, heron-fashion; but the wings beat
less slowly than the heron's. Small birds mob its journey,
possibly imagining a harrier. In Britain for nearly half a
century egg-thief and cartridge-maniac made an end of the
bittern and his nesting platform; in Australia—where 'the
Boomer' is guessed to have been at the back of the bunyip
fable—he deserves every protection.

BROWN BITTERN

NATURAL SIZE 28"   *Reproduced about 1/8 natural size*

167

WHITE EGRET *Egretta alba*

RECOGNITION: Aus. Immaculate heron-sized wader; golden-yellow bill. (3)

DESCRIPTION: 30-35. Flawless white; beak yellow, in breeding season black, greenish skin at base; legs black; iris yellow.

The big White Crane, moving with scrupulous care among the rushes of a lake or swamp, has a neck more kinked than the herons, to whose family it belongs and whose habits it shares. In pursuit of fish, tadpoles and frogs, White Egrets stand thigh-deep in water, a look of intense concentration even about the arched back. Suddenly the frozen pose is broken and the bright bill lunges home. Grassland around a lagoon or dam the egrets are hunting is combed for grasshoppers, lizards, and whatever the soggy turf may yield, the neck held curved, but elongated at intervals for stricter study of the ground. They are uneasy if watched for long and may rise; the head is then retracted to the shoulders and the legs outstretched behind the stumpy tail. When the bird is launched, the pinions moving deliberately and the primaries spread, an observer has time to admire the plumage, as unblemished as the morning air. This tall bird wears plumes on the back in the breeding season; but it was mainly the Little or Plumed Egret which was wiped out, colony after colony, when the millinery trade in the last century, in imitation of Eastern fineries, began loading hats with aigrettes. Today many countries safeguard these beautiful species, reinforced in northern Australia recently by the Cattle Egret. The newcomer from Asia, a parasite-ridder attendant on herds, is twenty inches long and of entirely white plumage.

WHITE EGRET

NATURAL SIZE 30″-35″   *Reproduced about 1/8 natural size*

STRAW-NECKED IBIS *Threskiornis spinicollis*

RECOGNITION: Aus. Black, long down-curved bill; white under; white tail shows flying. (3)

DESCRIPTION: 30. Upper parts black; under parts and neck white; spiny straw-tinted feathers on breast separated by black band from white abdomen; bare skin on head and face and down-curved bill black; legs red and grey-black; iris dark brown.

In that well-watered region, the Murray Basin, Pasture Protection Boards and other authorities have voiced fears that this fine Australian ibis may become as rare as the species anciently worshipped in Lower Egypt. Swamp drainage and tidying up of rivers is limiting the breeding grounds of this most valuable bird. Property owners seldom remember that for the most part local birds are their unpaid casual labourers; but on the whole they do respect the ibis for good work against the grasshopper. Usefulness apart, an ibis flock is a spectacle. It is magnificent when the great oval wings, with their span of nearly four feet, are spread and the birds glide high in a loosely-changing formation through the bland air of evening. On the ground the Straw-necked Ibis will follow the plough. More typically he is found busy in pastures or shallow lagoons, the big bill glistening with water as, with mandibles slightly apart, he prods repeatedly for crustaceans and other organisms. Sunlight picks up purple, green and bronze lights on the mantle.

STRAW–NECKED IBIS

NATURAL SIZE 30″   *Reproduced about 1/8 natural size*

171

WHITE IBIS   *Threskiornis molucca*

RECOGNITION: Aus., except most of south-west. White; black
head, neck and rump; sickle bill. (3)

DESCRIPTION: 30. White; neck and bare skin on face and head
black; back of head and nape pink markings; wing
quills, legs and bill black; iris red-brown.

The habits of the White Ibis do not differ from those of the
dark-mantled relatives with which it sometimes feeds. It may
once have preferred the lonelier lakes and reaches of pastoral
streams, but protection has brought increasing confidence.
Four White Ibises seen on Cairns golf course, for example,
thought the afternoon was as much their's as the players. On
the swamp the dark wing-termination distinguishes this ibis;
it gives the semblance of a black tail. When the birds are no
longer hungry they perch on favourite trees, stroll about grass
near water or rest sociably with waders on a raised bank or
islet, now and then extending the wings high above the back,
a languorous stretching motion. Isolated birds stand like white
landmarks in the midst of a paddock far distant from water as
they industriously free the ground of insects and their larvae.
The breeding rookeries, in northern Victoria for example, are
still eager objectives for foreign ornithologists, but the
wonder of overwhelming abundance has gone. Not much
more than fifty years ago a concourse of close on a quarter
of a million ibises was described. Now habitat is steadily
curtailed in the name of the 'rural economy' and Australia
finally may have to retrieve its 'wetlands' by re-purchase, as
the United States is doing.

WHITE IBIS

NATURAL SIZE 30″   *Reproduced about 1/8 natural size*

173

ROYAL SPOONBILL   *Platalea regia*

RECOGNITION: Aus. Long, broad, flattened bill, black, tip widening into 'spoon'; legs black. (3)

DESCRIPTION: 30. Plumage white; bill and legs slatey black; iris red-brown.

'Shoveler' was the old English name for the spoonbill, yet 'scyther' might have been better, for the curious bill is swept through water with a semi-circular, side-to-side motion to scoop in frogs, small fish, worms, molluscs, yabbies and other mud-frequenting creatures. This bird's habits are royal mostly in a Henry-the-Eighth, gluttonous sense. As it wallows in an oozy channel, soiled with mud and intent on food, an unkind description would be an avian pig in a sty—the comparison being kept up by the low, deep grunt the bird may give as it takes to the air. Once risen, the spoonbill begins to look more regal. The flight is regular and heavy, the outstretched neck slightly sagging and the legs in line; the big bird may mount to great heights, soaring and lazily turning on wide, still wings until it becomes a speck even in the binocular. During the pairing period a crest adornment develops. Apparently the Royal is more of a stay-at-home in his marsh drains and soggy acres than his yellow-billed congener, which I have come across numbers of times in scattered pastures carrying a dam.

ROYAL SPOONBILL

NATURAL SIZE 30″   *Reproduced about 1/8 natural size*

YELLOW-BILLED SPOONBILL   *Platalea flavipes*

RECOGNITION: Aus. Spatulate-ended bill and legs yellow. (3)

DESCRIPTION: 35. Plumage white; bill yellow; legs whitish-yellow; whitish bare skin, narrowly outlined black, forms mask about eye and forehead; iris white.

This larger spoonbill may be found with the Royal, standing with one leg tucked up or advancing slowly with high steps through the shallows, now and then suspending one foot contemplatively in mid-stride. It enjoys idly dozing in the sunshine at the edge of water and is slightly more lethargic in manner than its black-billed associate; it may incline to feed less by day. If the gathering of waders happens to include egrets, it will be noticed the spoonbill plumage is not a comparably dazzling white, but has something like the tinge of a sheet laundered with washing blue. The spoonbill family is watchful, but not secretive. The birds feed well into the open in swamps and lagoons; and in irrigation districts, where canals lie close to the road, a motorist who pulls up quietly can often have a close and prolonged view. He may possibly find when he raises his eyes that he, too, is being inspected by a spoonbill perched spectacularly on a bare tree.

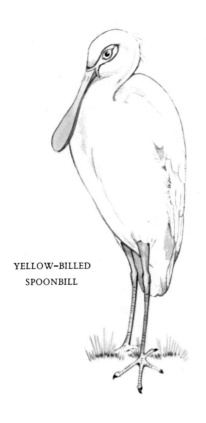

YELLOW-BILLED
SPOONBILL

NATURAL SIZE 35"   *Reproduced about 1/8 natural size*

PIED or WHITE-HEADED STILT   *Himantopus leucocephalus*

RECOGNITION: Aus. Very long-legged and long-billed bird, black-and-white study, except for purplish legs. (3).

DESCRIPTION: 15. Back and above and below wings, nape and slightly up-turned bill, black; shoulders and rest of plumage, white; legs bluish-red; iris, red-black. *Young*, sketchily grey on head and neck.

The abnormal length of the legs engages one first, then the abnormally long bill and finally the clean particularity of the pied plumage, neat and 'just so'. The bird has an ingenuous air: the round eye, almost centrally placed in the white head, looks at a quiet observer with timid friendliness. When wading —the three toes placed forward are slightly webbed—the legs seem to flex almost any way from the knee. The search for freshwater snails and the like is not a dogged head-down hunt; the bird, with swift, delicate motions of the head and neck, proceeds intuitively, like a diviner: bill and feet might have the acuteness of a blind man's fingertips. Food is eaten fastidiously. In the Northern Territory, one bird picked up a worm, which was shaken, soaked, washed in water and prepared for a best part of a minute before being swallowed. The stiffly-held legs, projecting behind in flight, still leave the stilt looking three-quarters leg and one-quarter bird. These waders feign death, or something that might be a swoon, when eggs or young seem threatened. Whole companies of the closely related Black-winged Stilt have been seen to sink in agonized mass collapse, but contrived to avoid uneven stones which would have made the 'death-bed' uncomfortable.

PIED STILT

NATURAL SIZE 15″   *Reproduced about 1/4 natural size*

BANDED STILT *Cladorhynchus leucocephalus*

RECOGNITION: Aus. Wide chestnut band across breast. (4,3)

DESCRIPTION: 15. Upper tail coverts and wings brown-black, white on secondaries; broad band of chestnut encloses breast, descending as darker line down abdomen; remainder white; legs pink; bill black; iris brown. *Young*, no band.

Not quite so leggy as the Pied Stilt, the Banded Stilt can be identified, if the chestnut cordon is not seen, by the absence of black about the neck. Much more at home in salt or brackish water than the other stilt, the banded bird sometimes wades too deeply for the chest decoration to be noted. Calls are akin to those of the Pied Stilt, a terrier-like bark and a piping whistle. Few nesting colonies of the Banded Stilt have been found, and then only in the interior, notably a very large company on Lake Callabonna in the north of South Australia. In Western Australia the prevalence of the birds on Rottnest Island has gained them a local name, 'Rottnest Snipe'. They fly and run swiftly, but are not swimmers. The Banded Stilts' elegance and beautiful markings did not protect them in former days from being shot and brought with other wildfowl to table.

BANDED STILT

NATURAL SIZE 15"   *Reproduced about 1/4 natural size*

SPUR-WINGED PLOVER   *Lobibyx novae-hollandiae*

RECOGNITION: Q'ld, south-eastern and central Aus., Tas. 'Alarm Bird'—raucous, skirling notes; yellow facial wattle. (3,4)

DESCRIPTION: 14. Upper parts brown-grey, wing quills darker; crown, nape, black; tail white banded black; under parts, throat, cheek, white; black markings side of chest; facial wattle in front of eye and base of beak, yellow; horny spur on wing-shoulder; legs reddish; bill and iris, yellow.

This watchful bird of the swamps, creeks and estuaries stands a handsomely-clad sentry for other feeders. At the first cause of uneasiness it twists away on rapid wings, with dinning, demonstrative cries as urgent as a car hooter. Although the alarm of many birds is ignored by other species, the Spurwing's stampede is promptly infectious. In the field the curious horny shoulder-spur may not be visible, but the yellow head-wattle is obvious. For all the neat brightness of the dress, Spurwings, like most plovers, have an obliterative plumage; when standing frozen, as the birds may for a moment before bolting, they blend well with the muddy background of a tidal river or the tints of the grasses on its banks. Spurwings eat crabs, yabbies, insects and herbage and are noisiest at sundown and sunrise. Flocks of a score or more forage together at night, when creaking calls and loud warning choruses intersperse with their feeding. When the flock has split into pairs the searcher for the nest among the tussocks has to admire the plover's combativeness. But as in most avian blitzes, the dives on an intruder, backed by a great racket, are not pressed to dangerous contact.

SPUR–WINGED PLOVER

NATURAL SIZE 14″   *Reproduced about 1/4 natural size*

183

EASTERN SWAMPHEN   *Porphyrio melanotus*

RECOGNITION: Aus. except south-west. Purplish, bulky bird; thick red bill and shield; white scut. (3)

DESCRIPTION: 18. Mantle and wings black; under parts purplish to midnight blue; under tail coverts white; bill and frontal plate red; legs ruddy pink, dusky band at knee; iris red.

Among the reeds on swamps, lagoons and often quite modest patches of water the white of the Swamphen's stumpy, convulsively jerked tail may give away its presence; or the first glimpse may be the brilliant-hued Roman nose and coloured forehead peeping between close stems. This sumptuous-looking, if ungainly, bird is not shy. Presently it will slowly sally out, the little red eyes peering, to wade in the shallows, using its long toes to hold still the reed stems it strips or examines for insects and plant food. Segments are bitten off and swallowed with precision. Now and then the head is plunged below the surface and the whole heavy body thrown almost off balance by the vigour of the bird's probing and dredging in the mud. Finding is not always keeping— there may be some altercation with the hen (grey and dowdy beside her imperially-dressed mate) over what has been brought to light, for swamphens are fractious, as well as lumbering. They fly rather jerkily, the legs at first dangling, perhaps advertising the move by honking and shrilling cries. The Western Swamphen has clear blue on the breast and is browner above, the legs sometimes being green. Swamphens will leave their reed cover to roost among trees, where unrestful noises advertise them during the night.

EASTERN SWAMPHEN

DUSKY MOORHEN *Gallinula tenebrosa*

RECOGNITION: Aus. except north-western and Central and N.T.
Black, with red forehead shield. White tail patches;
tail constantly flirted, swimming and walking. (3)

DESCRIPTION: 14½. Black, tinted brown; under tail coverts white;
base of bill and frontal plate red, tip of bill yellow;
legs and feet green, red 'garter' above knee (heel);
iris brown-red.

Moorhen is a corruption of 'mere-hen'. 'Waterhen' is the alternative sometimes heard, for a pair may be found on any river, swamp, lake or pool big enough for residence. The birds like sedges and reed cover and hug the bank more than coots do. More time, too, is passed on land, the moorhen picking its way with long strides and lifting its feet high; the quest for seeds and berries may take it far from water after dark, when its loud 'Prruk!' is startling. The white patches at the side of the tail are prominent when the moorhen is jerkily swimming or walking; the tail is smartly flirted and the head bobs. In the water, where aquatic plants are eaten, moorhens do not herd together like the coots; they dive far less frequently and rather better; if watched they may swim with only the bill emerging. At an alarm the moorhen patters and panics over the surface, rises a little and flies limply into cover. Bouts of battle at pairing time are more vindictive than the coot's; a worsted male may be in a bad plight. With its pert looks and its calls—some harsh and metallic, some soft and coaxing— the Moorhen adds interest to any sheet of water. It is commonly found on park lakes where comfortable cover has been allowed to grow.

DUSKY MOORHEN

NATURAL SIZE 14½″   *Reproduced about 1/4 natural size*

COOT *Fulica atra*

RECOGNITION: Aus. Black, with white forehead shield. Nearly always on water, swims with head jerking; noisy. (3)

DESCRIPTION: 15. Plumage, shades of black and slate grey; bill and frontal plate white tinged mauve at close view; legs grey or greenish; iris red.

The Coot, with his obvious white badge, lives on rivers and inland water expanses, often gathering in large numbers—for he is at the same time sociable and combative. Fights may start not only when territory is being reserved, but at any season; the rivals swim at each other in a dour, crouching posture, then angled high in the water, 'let fly' with beak and wing. There is much raucous commotion and splashing till honour is satisfied—usually before any serious injury has been done. The Coot's observations on his world are varied and obstreperous—honking and clinking sounds, with an approach to a shriek or whistle. He dives industriously for water herbs, small fish and molluscs, disappearing with a splash for a few seconds and re-appearing possibly at a distance, because his lobed feet carry him fast under water. Whether paddling along, the head mechanically bobbing, scuttling over the surface half-flying, half-running, landing with a smack, or poking around on awkward legs for grass and berries along the bank, the Coot fails to look accomplished or handy. A hint of clumsiness remains in the flight. The birds fly straight and fairly fast with an effect of urgent effort, the legs and heavy feet trailing behind the tail. Coots assemble at estuaries, but enjoy fresh water more than salt.

COOT

CRESTED GREBE   *Podiceps cristatus*

RECOGNITION: Aus. Slender, long-necked, sharp-beaked; tufts on crown, and cape of elongated feathers round upper neck. (3)

DESCRIPTION: 21. Upper parts grey-brown, grey-black on ear tufts surmounting head, and on back of neck; under parts and cheeks satin white; frill round neck rich chestnut, tipped black; bill horn; legs yellowish-olive; iris crimson; no tail. *Young*, ash-brown, striped neck.

'Tippet Grebe' was a common name in the days when women demanded the breast feathers. Another is 'Loon', for their courtship frolics make these divers the equivalent of the 'mad March hare'. One of the spring-time rituals is for a pair to approach each other with necks outstretched; straightening them, they rear up, front touching front, gently revolving and parrying strokes of each other's bill and at intervals bending back their slim necks almost to the spine. This grebe, with its distinctive head-dress, prefers ample room on a fair-sized lake or reservoir; he generally keeps a distance from the bank. The nest, a raft of vegetation secured to rushes, lily-pads or like moorings, is built well beyond interfering reach. The diver disappears for fish and other water prey with a swift 'well-oiled' motion and can stay down for nearly half a minute. Below water the legs ply together. On top, the grebe floats low, neck relaxed when he is idle, but stiffly upright for purposeful swimming. Growling and rasping notes are used in the breeding season and one call, 'Jik, jik', carries far over the water. The young at first ride on the backs of their parents, who swim with conscious care.

CRESTED GREBE

NATURAL SIZE 21″   *Reproduced about 1/4 natural size*

PELICAN *Pelecanus conspicillatus*

RECOGNITION : Aus. Enormous beak development distinguishes from other birds. (3,4)

DESCRIPTION : 60. White, with wing edges, stumpy tail and lower back black. Slight crest, or mane, grey; bill and naked membrane of pouch pinky flesh-colour; legs and bare skin about eye yellow to buff; iris brown.

These imposing fishermen assemble on lagoons, lakes, swamps, rivers and estuaries. Sometimes the flocks, which may be hundreds strong, make excursions well out to sea; but normally the Pelican likes the shallows where he can sweep the bottom with his flexible lower mandible, up to eighteen inches in length, with its sub-joined elastic 'landing-net' pouch. Pelicans will form an arc to shepherd fish into water a few inches deep where they can be taken easily; on the Coorong I have seen them thrashing the sea surface with their wings to hasten the round-up. After a meal the birds waddle ashore to digest and preen, their land progress full of clumsy complication compared with their buoyant swimming and easy power on the wing. When he goes aloft, showing a wing-span greater than a Wedge-tailed Eagle's, the Pelican is one of the rulers of the winds. The bulky body, with head tucked close to the shoulders, is a picture of compact force. The birds move in V-pattern and line-ahead, the files often appearing to take rhythm from the leader; or the concourse may rise and circle very high, drifting inland as a simmering black and white cloud. When they re-appear they regain the water, braking with their feet and taking station in extended order.

PELICAN

NATURAL SIZE 60″   *Reproduced about 1/15 natural size*

193

AUSTRALIAN GANNET *Sula serrator*

RECOGNITION: Off-shore, southward from Brisbane round to Perth. Large sailing white bird, black wing-tips; plummets from height into sea. (4)

DESCRIPTION: 32–38. White, except for blackish primaries—about quarter of wing from tip shows black in flight—and four blackish centre tail feathers; head, straw yellow; legs slatey, lined yellow on toes; bill slate grey; iris light grey. *Young*, mottled greyish-brown and white.

The Gannet is one of the grandest ocean birds and one of the easiest to admire; it is frequently sighted off-shore, sometimes in scores. Probably the gannets will be fishing; it is the spectacular plunge into the sea from a hundred and fifty feet or more, and the column of spray thrown up by the impact, that catch the eye. Superb flyers, they cruise in spacious curves and circles at uniform speed, three or four beats of the pinions merging into long glides. When prey is spotted they check pace by shooting vertically upwards, wheel, fix the target, half close the wings and drop like rocks, the wings being completely shut just before the shock of the dive. For some seconds the gannet stays below, while the fish is swallowed; then, surfacing, floats for a moment. A few arduous strokes lift him back on patrol. Sometimes shoals are attacked in oblique dashes from about twenty-five feet. When a gale drives the food supply deep and the rollers are slamming in with whistling tops, the gannet's flight is no less wonderful. The big birds move into the storm in a low undulating line, just clear of the waves' turmoil, as though they were part of the buffeting wind and tumbling waters.

AUSTRALIAN
GANNET

NATURAL SIZE 32"-38"   *Reproduced about 1/8 natural size*

BLACK CORMORANT   *Phalacrocorax carbo*

RECOGNITION: Aus. Biggest cormorant; black, white face patch and, in breeding season, white patch on thighs. (4,3)

DESCRIPTION: 35. Black, glossed green; purple and bronze lights on mantle; lower face and chin white, and white nuptial patch on thigh obvious in flight; bill horn, yellower at base; bare skin around eye yellow; legs blue-black; iris sea-green. *Young*, brownish, under parts whitish.

The cormorant—'Shag' in Australian usage—is a sea and shore bird first, but also fishes in rivers, lakes and quite small dams. Over water it usually skims the surface with strong, even wing-beats; over land it may set a high course, wheeling and soaring with almost hawk-like grace. Under water it progresses with a jerky swiftness: a fish must be fast to outpace the dark shadow propelled by simultaneous hard-driving backstrokes of the feet. Normally the capture is whisked to the top and the fight knocked out of a too-game fish by a rude shaking and battering on the surface. The meal may appear as uncomfortably large as the prey a snake contrives to swallow. The cormorant dives glibly, with a quick preparatory half vault. If suspicious it sinks till only head and neck project, periscope-fashion. After working spells the diver sits square on a rock or post with stiffly-elbowed wings, to dry his feathers—more pervious to water than those of most aquatic birds. The posture reminds one of a church lectern. Fishermen like to blame their expert competitor for shortages of species eaten by humans; but their grumbling is not borne out by many thorough investigations. The hoarse cormorant croak, the only note, is heard mostly at nesting time. Colonies are likely to be scented before they are seen.

BLACK
CORMORANT

NATURAL SIZE 35″   *Reproduced about 1/8 natural size*

PIED CORMORANT *Phalacrocorax varius*

RECOGNITION: Aus. Commonest and largest black and white coastal cormorant; naked skin in front of eye, orange. Glistening plumage. (4)

DESCRIPTION: 31. Upper parts black, bronze-green gloss; cheeks, front and side of neck and under parts, white; in front of eye skin orange or yellow, below blue-green; legs black; bill dark horn; iris green. *Young*, upper parts brown, under parts white and brown.

This cormorant and the Black Cormorant look much of a size and their habits and haunts are similar. The pied bird cares less to come inland and does not soar with the Black Cormorant's abandon. At the coast Pied Cormorants may gather in big numbers; their formation-flying is direct and low on the face of the water. The White-breasted Cormorant (27), found along the southern coast and around Tasmania, may be told apart by the blackish-purple naked skin of the face. The Little Pied Cormorant, (23) Aus., is smaller than other white-fronted cormorants; its bill is shorter and it is more often met about inland waters and swamps. It dives with great adroitness. The Little Black Cormorant, (24) Aus., is also a species frequently seen inland. Its lesser size distinguishes it from the Black Cormorant; the pouch and naked skin of the face are dark, not orange.

PIED CORMORANT

NATURAL SIZE 31″   *Reproduced about* 1/8 *natural size*

PACIFIC GULL   *Gabianus pacificus*

RECOGNITION: Southern coast, eastern and western coasts to Tropic of Capricorn, Tas. Ponderous; black back; heavy, deep yellow bill. (4)

DESCRIPTION: 25. White; back, wings and sub-terminal tail band black; legs yellow; bill yellow, tipped red; iris white, rimmed yellow. *Young*, mottled brown; legs dark brown.

This overbearing gull with a wing-span of about five feet is seldom sighted inland. It lords it over the foreshore, beating and sailing with confident deliberation, tyrannically thrusting aside smaller feeders from any promising meal. In looks and manners it strongly resembles the Great Black-backed Gull of the northern hemisphere, a bandit which is five inches bigger and is sometimes termed the vulture of the sea. One habit the two share is to fly to twenty or thirty feet in order to drop molluscs on rock to smash the shells—the Great Black-backed Gull has been seen to treat in the same fashion sea birds it has half killed. Pacific Gulls, usually alone or in pairs, reduce Silver Gulls standing near to slightness. In the dappled immature plumage—as with most gull species adult dress requires about four years—they appear even larger, although this is a trick of the eye. Heavily-armed pirates, Pacific Gulls are omnivorous and uneasy neighbours for waders and weaker birds of the shore-line. They show some preference for carrion flesh, no matter how 'ancient and fishlike' and come boldly scavenging when a catch is being gutted. The dark juveniles are 'mollymawks' or 'mollymokes' (words mangled from Dutch) to the crews of fishing boats, or the term may be 'molly-hawk', a name seamen apply impartially to gulls, skuas, petrels and the smaller albatrosses.

PACIFIC GULL

NATURAL SIZE 27″   *Reproduced about 1/8 natural size*

SILVER GULL *Larus novae-hollandiae*

RECOGNITION: Aus. Legs and bill red; more common than Pacific Gull. (4)

DESCRIPTION: 16. White; mantle·pearl grey; outer primaries black with white 'mirrors' near tip, remainder white with black band near tip; legs and bill brown to clear red; iris white, rimmed red. *Young*, mottled brown; legs and bill black.

An ornamental bird, Australia's only small gull is common about the coasts throughout the year; loosely-joined bands fly, rest and noisily quest together for food. The Silver maintains the customary gull patrol, flapping, gliding and wheeling back and forth over beach and water in reconnoitring flight, alert for any morsel to stoke its competitive energy. Much time is wasted in futile scrums and chases to wrest a tit-bit from the first claimant; 'priority' is not a word that has spread to gulls. The sea is watched for small surface swimmers, but the Silver is not an expert diver. It fills out its provender with almost any mouthful, dead or alive, the tide turns up. It is a helpful scavanger, but a persistent egg-thief. Nesting 'gulleries' may be established on the coast or inland and the birds will haunt fresh water remote from the sea. The voice is by turns truculent, querulous and strident; a harsh 'Kee-ar' is one note, and prolonged yelping protests—the birds standing hunched with indignation—accompany recriminations over the ownership of a catch. When attacking minor surface prey gulls flounce down feet first, so offering their legs to large fish likewise preying on a shoal. A cripple hopping about the beach is a commonplace and no doubt the kindly offerings of picnickers help the disabled to survive.

SILVER GULL

NATURAL SIZE 16″   *Reproduced about 1/4 natural size*

CASPIAN TERN *Hydroprogne caspia*

RECOGNITION: Aus. Strong vermilion bill, black cap; beats, hovers and dives. (4)

DESCRIPTION: 21. Upper parts ash grey, wing primaries. dark grey, tail coverts white; cap and nape black, streaky in winter; under parts white; bill bright red, dark at tip; legs and iris black. *Young*, cap streaked; bill yellowish-brown; legs brown.

Size alone—the Caspians are as big as crows—distinguishes this heavily built sea-swallow as it combs the shallows, its head watchfully down, the long, pointed wings irregularly beating with down-strokes that are incisive and forceful. From time to time the patrol checks. With short, slightly forked tail expanded stiffly, wings steeply raised and fanning, bill pointed at the likely prey, the bird pauses; then screws obliquely seawards and is on the small surfacing fish with a splash. In a moment the tern will be climbing again. A swimming shoal may collect a strident tern company, plunging and careening in a hurried traffic. The sounds then uttered seem too jarring and harsh for such decorative, aerial forms; they make plain why 'Screecher' is one name for the bird in its European range. Nests are sometimes solitary, sometimes in small colonies on the ground near the sea; and human, animal or bird intruders may have to fend off dive-bombing as purposeful as any magpie's. Occasional birds pay visits to inland water. This sea-swallow, the biggest of the tern race, is a citizen of the oceans and nests as far north as the Baltic. Terns anciently were believed to be a sort of gull and how the separate name arose is not known. The Danish 'terne' and 'taerne', the Norse 'terna' and the Swedish 'tarna' have been said to have bearing—but why, when all those words mean 'maid-servant'?

CASPIAN TERN

NATURAL SIZE 21″   *Reproduced about 1/7 natural size*

MOUNTAIN DUCK or CHESTNUT-BREASTED
SHELDUCK   *Casarca tadornoides*

RECOGNITION: Southern Aus., Tas. and N.S.W. Starch-white collar, golden breast; in flight, clear-cut black and white. (3,4)

DESCRIPTION: 25. Head and upper neck black, with bottle-green sheen; collar white; base of neck and breast chestnut; back, belly and tail black; abdomen with rufous bars; green gloss on tail; wing secondary coverts white, outer secondaries green, inner chestnut; underwing white; bill and legs almost black; iris brown. *Female*, 23, white around eye and at base of bill; colouring generally less emphatic.

The Mountain Duck, which denies its name by haunting estuaries, lakes, flats, moist pastures and sometimes farm dams, is, except for the Musk Duck (which behaves more like a diver than flyer) the largest of the Australian duck tribe. It has not only size, but dignity—the contained air of a dandy; 'the pride of Australian waters', said Sturt. Mountain Ducks in big gatherings make a debonair assembly; but more often the birds are seen in pairs, when the female's quieter costume and lesser size are obvious. She resembles a plump, deferential companion out with a gallant. While she eats along the herbage of the water-line, the drake stands close guard, erectly glancing round, uneasy if there is a spectator, but disdaining to make off unless there is real danger. At last he gives the low, gurgling signal to retire. When all appears serene, the duck may take her trick as sentinel. The Mountain Duck is also known as the Chestnut-breasted Shelduck, or Sheldrake—the prefix has nothing to do with shield: it means pied. The birds, happily for them, are coarse and pungent eating.

MOUNTAIN DUCK

NATURAL SIZE 25″   *Reproduced about 1/8 natural size*

BLACK or GREY DUCK *Anas superciliosa*

RECOGNITION: Aus. White lines above eye and from base of bill to back of eye; uniformly drab colouring. (3)

DESCRIPTION: 19-23. Body feathers dull dark brown, with narrow buff edging; white V-lines on head; throat and underwing whitish; legs dull green-yellow; bill lead-blue; iris brown.

A duck that is sometimes called Black, sometimes Grey and sometimes Brown may be rightly suspected to show no dominant colour. The only adornment of the Black Duck (to use its most common name) is the unobtrusive green of the speculum—the term for the oblong of glossy colour seen on the wing of many freshwater ducks. The bird's behaviour, apart from the odd contortions of courtship and the production of several, far from musical, quacking notes, is as self-effacing as its dress. As one of the shooter's main 'bags', it prefers to stay out of the limelight and in the ruck. During summer, when safe from all but gunners, a too-considerable number of whom ignore the close seasons appointed by the States, the Black Duck will come to water frequented by human beings and show a fairly tame disposition. The food consists of water plants, herbage, grass and the snails and small fry in and near water. In flight the pinions ply and whistle; the call note is a drawling 'Frank, Frank'. The courtship of this, the most widely distributed duck, includes spurts of swimming, mock preening and rearing perpendicularly out of the water, wings flapping, to 'model' the breeding dress. A seeming prevision is shown in the migration on the eve of the gunners' annual orgy to take sanctuary on lakes in the parks of capital cities.

BLACK *or* GREY DUCK

NATURAL SIZE 19″–23″   *Reproduced about 1/8 natural size*

WHITE-EYED DUCK   *Nyroca australis*

RECOGNITION: Aus. Mainly brown; white wing stripe salient in flight. (3).

DESCRIPTION: 20. Upper parts, head, breast and abdomen brown; broad white stripe on wing; lower breast, underwing and undertail, white; legs slate: bill blackish; iris white. *Female*, bill, no white tip, iris brown.

The White-eyed Duck is thoroughly wary and, once startled, fast in the air. It habitually gains its animal and vegetable food in the under-water mud, expertly going below for longish periods, vanishing sometimes with an upward spring and a head-first dive, sometimes slipping under without fuss. When taking wing, it beats the water surface as a runway for some distance, accelerating with feet and wings. On land this diving duck is distinctly awkward.

WOOD DUCK or MANED GOOSE   *Chenonetta jubata*

RECOGNITION: Aus. Mainly bluish-grey; green wing stripe between two white stripes. (3)

DESCRIPTION: 19. Head and throat brown; black 'mane' feathers on nape; mantle and wing coverts grey, with quills black, and green stripe double-edged white; underwing white; breast flecked brown and white; flanks grey, barred brown; abdomen and undertail, dark brown; legs black; bill brown and short; iris brown. *Female*, wing quills brown; under parts white; duller green speculum.

The duck with the goose-like bill often feeds along the sides of streams and flies to search moist grassy levels lying some way from water. It may gather in strong flocks. Where watercourses are fringed by trees, the Maned Goose frequently takes a look-out perch among the boughs.

WHITE-EYED DUCK

WOOD DUCK

BLACK SWAN   *Cygnus atratus*

RECOGNITION: Aus., except areas in far north. Swimming, black; flying, trailing edge of wings broad white and long out-stretched neck; stormy, honking calls. (3,4)

DESCRIPTION: 36-40. Plumage black, flight quills white; legs dark grey; bill coral, white bar across upper mandible; iris red. *Young*, grey in down.

Fears have been voiced abroad that Western Australia's emblem—like another emblem, the kangaroo—might be exterminated, except as an ornamental captive. So far these noble birds remain, east and west, abundant; flocks may touch the thousand mark. The first sighting is a familiar tale. Vlamingh, the Dutch navigator, rubbed his eyes to meet a swan uncompromisingly, wrongfully black when he penetrated into Swan River, and he wisely took back to Batavia the live phenomenon to defend his story. To a world all snowy swans an opposite was incredible. Today domesticated parties of Australia's bird are admired in numerous countries and here we still have the free spectacle. In the air the flight quills become visible, indeed salient, showing as broad white borders to the outer wing. While the flock, or herd, is swimming, these contrasting feathers are not obvious. A crowd of cobs and pens disturbed on water take off with battering feet, with a surge of sound like mounting wind; and from taut, urgent necks their trumpetings drift throatily back. In his strenuous rush overhead or as he glides, soft as his reflection, on still water, the Black Swan is a bird of romance, deserving, like his white English counterpart, to be respected as a 'bird royal'.

BLACK SWAN

NATURAL SIZE 36″-40″   *Reproduced about* 1/10 *natural size*

INDEX

216

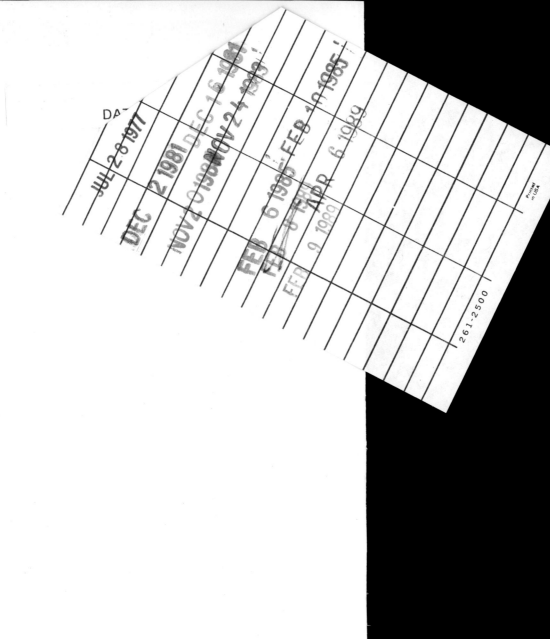